My So-Called Freelance Life

MY SO-CALLED Freelance LIFE

How to Survive and Thrive as a
Creative Professional for Hire

MICHELLE
GOODMAN

SEAL PRESS

My So-Called Freelance Life
How to Survive and Thrive as a Creative Professional for Hire

Copyright © 2008 by Michelle Goodman

Published by
Seal Press
A Member of Perseus Books Group
1700 Fourth Street
Berkeley, California

Library of Congress Cataloging-in-Publication Data

Goodman, Michelle, 1967-
  My so-called freelance life : how to survive and thrive as a creative professional for hire / by Michelle Goodman.
    p. cm.
  ISBN-13: 978-1-58005-259-7
  ISBN-10: 1-58005-259-2
  1. Self-employed. 2. Career development. I. Title.
  HD8036.G66 2008
  650.1—dc22

                          2008020825

Cover design by Kate Basart/Union Pageworks
Interior design by Megan Cooney
Printed in the United States of America
Distributed by Publishers Group West

For anyone who's ever hit the snooze button
five times in a row on Monday morning.

contents

PART 3

Your So-Called Freelance Life

"To fulfill a dream, to be allowed to sweat over lonely labor, to be given a chance to create, is the meat and potatoes of life. The money is the gravy."

—Bette Davis

"The two most beautiful words in the English language are 'check enclosed.'"

—Dorothy Parker

introduction

Eat, Pray, Quit

When I was twelve and writing in my diary about how much I hated my braces and loved Arthur Finkelstein, I fantasized about someday publishing the whole hot confessional mess. My book, *The Bride Wore a Night Brace,* would be acclaimed the world over.

Girls would write me sentimental notes about how I'd helped them learn to smile again, despite the ten pounds of hardware obscuring their teeth. Boys would send me lengthy missives about how I'd convinced them to take a second look at that gangly girl in the corner, the one who could pick up twelve different radio stations with her headgear, and ask her if she wanted to dance. High school teachers and college professors alike would make my treatise on preteen angst required reading in their classrooms. Politicians would buy it for their sons and daughters. I'd be invited to the White House, interviewed by Barbara Walters, and—once the movie version of my opus grossed a billion dollars—given my own star on Hollywood Boulevard.

Not for one minute did I think that someday I'd be trapped in a 9-to-5 (or 5-to-9) job, fielding thirty dozen emails a day and straining to stay awake during staff meetings. Not even for a nanosecond.

Then I finished school and cruel reality set in.

Occasionally, my older, wiser coworkers would stop debating whose carpal tunnel was worse long enough to share their hard-won pearls of workforce wisdom with me. "I used to be like you, thinking that one day I'd pursue my own writing or take up painting again," they'd say. "But eventually, you learn to let go of those silly dreams. You gotta grow up sometime and get a real job like everyone else."

Why? I remember thinking. What's so juvenile about actually liking what you do for a living? What's wrong with designing your own career if you can't stomach the one you've got or can't figure out what kind of

1

a job you want in the first place? Isn't that a better bet than hanging on to a 9-to-5 that makes you feel like you're crawling over broken glass sixty hours a week?

I'm guessing you can relate. You want more control over the work you do, who you do it for, and where you do it. You don't want to be told what the pay range for the job is—you want to set it yourself. You want a flexible schedule so you can devote more than fifteen minutes a day to your family, the canine couture empire you've been hoping to launch, or the screenplay you've been nursing for the past decade. You want to work in your bunny slippers with your dog lying at your feet. Most important, you want off the corporate hamster wheel and you want it now.

You certainly wouldn't be alone. Only one in two Americans are happy with their jobs, reports The Conference Board, one of the world's leading business think tanks. Not surprisingly, in 2007 the U.S. Census Bureau found that almost twenty-one million Americans work as self-employed professionals or independent contractors.

Some of us turn to freelancing in the wake of a layoff. Others turn to it as a way of easing back into the workforce after having a child. Others have simply found that traffic snarls cause them to froth at the mouth and fluorescent lighting gives them a bad rash.

This isn't one of those "I am perfect and you can be too" books where I tell you how rich and slick and esteemed and redeemed I am (don't I wish), or how I did everything right when I first fled the cube in 1992 (nothing could be further from the truth). If you've read my first book, *The Anti 9-to-5 Guide: Practical Career Advice for Women Who Think Outside the Cube,* a guide to fleeing the cube farm for flexible, temporary, overseas, social service, or self-employed work, you know I was hardly the poster child for self-employed success during my early freelance years. When I left my day job in the dust at age twenty-four, I had the business sense of a beagle, the paltriest of portfolios, only one client to my name, and no money saved.

Thanks to a crazy little thing called trial and error, I fortunately got with the freelancing program and figured out everything from naming my price and structuring my time to wooing clients and whipping my contracts into shape. To help you do the same (only without all that fumbling in the dark), I packed as much of my freelance know-how as would fit into this book. So consider this your crash course in becoming gainfully self-employed.

Every great story has three acts—even the story of your shiny new freelance life. In this book, I've laid out those acts for you chapter and verse. In Part 1, you'll find details on those first key steps you need to take as an indie professional, from making a budget and setting goals for yourself to getting a business license and building a web portfolio. In Part 2, we'll talk about landing the work, from marketing yourself like mad and getting in the referral game to negotiating rates and contracts like nobody's business. And in Part 3, we'll cover all the day-to-day details of surviving and thriving as a creative professional for hire—in other words, staying sane, solvent, and off the IRS's shit list.

Whether you're on a fact-finding mission, eager to learn how this newfangled way of boss-free working works, or already freelancing on the side and wondering how soon you can turn in your letter of resignation, this book is for you. Even the seasoned freelancers in the bunch are sure to pick up some tips and tricks here. After all, what freelancer doesn't love a little dirt on how her self-employed counterparts deal with missed deadlines, clients from hell, and checks that are MIA?

For the record, I'm not an accountant, financial adviser, or legal professional. I'm a journalism major turned freelance writer who makes her living writing articles, books, and corporate marketspeak, with the occasional editing or teaching gig thrown in for variety. While I touch on some of the legal and financial gobbledygook of working for yourself in these pages, my advice isn't meant to take the place of the advice of a trained financial or legal pro (in fact, my own legal adviser made me type this very sentence). So for tax, financial planning, and legal help, please, hire yourself a good accountant or lawyer who can keep you out of debt and out of jail, okay? Don't waste your one phone call from the pokey on me.

Instead, learn from my sixteen years of hard-won freelance wisdom and the missteps I made while scrambling to gain a foothold on my so-called freelance life. As far as I'm concerned, you might as well benefit from the biggest lessons I learned and blunders I made and save yourself some time, agita, and bounced checks in the process.

Because diversity is a beautiful thing, I've also included the war stories and sage advice from several dozen of my full-time freelance heroines (and a couple of moonlighters), from a pet photographer to a personal trainer, writer to web developer, visual artist to virtual assistant, rocker to radio producer, animator to auctioneer. Many of these freelancers are the main breadwinners in their households, regardless of whether they're single, shacked up, or somebody's mom. Many have mortgages and kids to put through college. All of them rely on their freelance income to make ends meet; you won't find any hobbyists or trust fund babies here.

To round out the discussion, you'll also hear from a handful of clients, financial pros, and legal eagles. And since no DIY career book would be complete without a little homework, you'll find a few exercises to do along the way (no deep breathing or "creative visualization" techniques—I promise!). So get out your pencils and Post-it notes, and get ready to dig in.

I realize that you may be afraid. Afraid of not having enough money to pay your bills. Afraid of giving up your health insurance and 401(k). Afraid no one will hire you. Afraid you'll go nuts working alone. Afraid you'll work all the time and have no life. Afraid you'll take the leap and your parachute won't open.

I was too when I started working solo. But I quickly learned that a little planning (and a whole lot of chutzpah) goes a long way, especially when it comes to chasing your freelance dreams and dealing with the financial realities of life without a steady paycheck.

So allow me to be your tour guide as you strive to get your so-called freelance life on track. Let me tell you what to do with those business card designs you've been sketching on the back of a pink "While You Were Out" notepad and how to transform that useless corner alcove into a fully functional home office. Because wanting to make a living as a freelance cartoonist, clothing designer, or computer programmer isn't silly. It's dreamable, doable, and damn good fun.

What's silly is giving up the dream because some overworked officemate who lives to bitch about her carpal tunnel syndrome said you should. Now enough stalling, let's get to work.

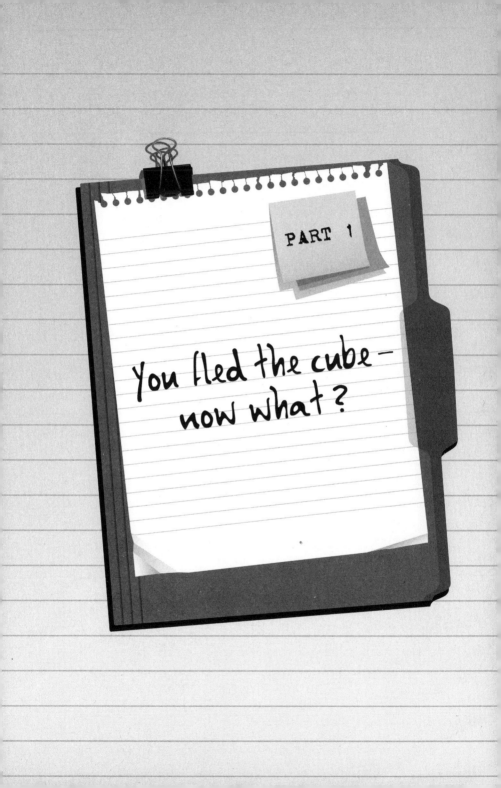

PART 1

You fled the cube —
now what?

F reelancing isn't just about selling your talents, advice, or wares. Working for yourself as a creative professional also means playing chief executive, bean counter, sales rep, marketing maven, tech support, contract manager, and admin assistant.

Or, as author and journalist Lynn Harris puts it, "People think that freelancers sort of sit at their desks all day and just have ideas. But we're running a business. It's a business I can run in my socks, but it's a business."

While I'm all about running the best possible business one can run in her socks, I'm not about doing things the traditional (tedious, expensive) way. Business plans that double as paperweights? No thanks. Three-thousand-dollar executive desk/hutch/swivel chair set? Not on your life. Instead, I'll give you the quick-and-dirty list of what you need to consider and do right away to get this freelance party started—and what plans, purchases, and services you can back-burner till your business grows a smidge bigger.

In a perfect world, you'd plan, ramp up, and build your freelance business on the side while keeping a steady paycheck. After all, if you quit your day job today, it's highly unlikely you'll have a full freelance workload tomorrow. But not everyone has ten to twenty spare hours a week to moonlight. And many creative professionals find themselves diving into the freelance pool headfirst after getting laid off, becoming a parent, or getting so fed up with their 9-to-5 they accidentally blurt out where their boss can stick it. If you count yourself among that crowd, not to worry. Many freelancers before you have started their solo careers without a lick of planning and lived to tell the tale (yours truly included). With the help of this book, you'll be a lean, mean, freelancing machine in no time.

Even if you've been freelancing on the side or full-time for a few years, you're going to find some useful pointers here. As creative pros for hire, it's easy for us to get caught up with the project work on our plate but gloss over the business side of things. If your website, office space, or income could use a makeover, this section will serve up some suggestions. And if you're bored with your current workload, these chapters could give you the kick in the pants you need to shake things up.

Chapter 1

Business Plan To Go
Even Thumper had goals

"Smart kid like you. You got to have a plan. Some kind of a dream."

—Peter Gallagher in *The O.C.*, 2003

I used to think business plans were for people who preferred pumps and pearls to slippers and sweats. When I started working for myself as a freelancer, I wasn't looking for a bank loan or an angel investor, so, I figured, why would I need some wonky thirty-page tome? How the heck was a hefty mission statement going to help an independent professional like me land better clients and make enough money to pay my rent?

Then I was asked to write a story on business plans for *NAFE Magazine*, a publication aimed at female execs. In the interviews I gathered for the article, business guru after business guru griped about the way so many self-employed people operate on autopilot, leaping at every opportunity that falls into their laps—the good, the bad, and the ugly, intention and ambition be damned.

Melissa Krinzman, who runs Venture Architects, a New York–based firm that helps entrepreneurs looking for seed money develop their business plans, said something that stuck with me: "A business plan helps you focus on selecting the client rather than waiting for the client to select you."

In other words, commit to paper your latest and greatest freelance goals—why you want to work for yourself in the first place, and what projects and clients you hope to land in the process—and you liberate yourself from thinking you have to jump on every gig that comes your way.

A Cure for the Common Waffler

I'm a waffler at heart. Show me a decision that needs making and I'll show you a woman capable of flip-flopping three dozen times in the course of an hour. You might say I'm a lot like Tevye, the lead character in the musical *Fiddler on the Roof*. Gifted with the ability to examine any situation from about nineteen different angles, Tevye was freakishly fond of the phrase "on the other hand."

Dangle a sweet-sounding gig in my face, and you'll witness this modern-day Freelancer on the Roof in action: Let's say HotShitStartup .com contacts me out of the blue and offers me serious cash to write web copy for the next two weeks about some newfangled wireless gizmo I don't give a whit about. In deciding whether to take the job, my thought process might go something like this:

> *Hmmmm, wasn't HotShitStartup.com just on the front page of the business section? That gig suuuue would look spiffy on my resume. On the other hand, I'm so over high-tech corporate work; didn't I swear it off back in 2007 (and 2006, and 2005)? On the other hand, the pay is phenomenal—twice as much as I've made on any other project this year. On the other hand, if I take the gig, I'll have to burn the midnight oil since I already have four magazine articles due this month. On the other hand, it'd be cool to have this new client in the hopper in case I ever need some high-paying tech work to fall back on. On the other hand, I already have enough dull-as-dirt corporate work to fall back on . . .*

And that's just in the first fifteen minutes.

That's why the idea of getting my goals down on paper resonates with me. Regardless of whether you're a waffler, if you want to work solo, you too need a written game plan—what I like to call a Business Plan To Go. It doesn't have to be *War and Peace*; the CliffsNotes version will do just fine. All you need is a short list of your freelance goals for the year—a roadmap of where you want your career to go, and some directions for how to get there. It might be all of three hundred words. It might be posted on your blog. It might be scrawled on the back of a beer coaster. Point is, jotting down your freelance hopes, along with your to-do list for making those dreams a reality, will help remind you why you're here, working at home in hot pink pajamas with three-day unwashed hair (or, uh, maybe that's just me).

Keeping my one-page plan tacked to the wall above my desk ensures that the next time HotShitStartup.com calls, I won't get bogged down with all that Tevye-like indecision. Instead, I'll glance at the game plan I wrote long before some flashy webpreneurs with deep pockets began parading a wheelbarrow of carrots in front of me, and I'll assess. Quickly. *Sure, this sounds like a great gig, but is it a great gig for me, given what I want to accomplish this year?* If the answer is no, I won't take the gig; if the gig isn't in line with my overall freelance goals and I'm not starved for work, why derail my creative hopes and dreams for the next few weeks or months?

Here's an example, one of the biggest goals from my own Business Plan To Go for 2008:

WRITE FOR MORE NATIONAL PUBLICATIONS.
Game plan:

1. Introduce myself to the editors of *Fancypants Magazine* and FiftyMillionEyeballsOnYourWriting.com, whose names a couple of freelance friends kindly passed along over the holidays.

2. Pitch an article to any of the aforementioned editors who take the bait.

3. Continue filling my story-idea well by actually reading those online press release and news alert services I've subscribed to (Newswise, Google).

4. Write one new humor essay a quarter and shop it around with doctor's-office-worthy publications.

❺ Limit corporate gigs to one a month, if that. If I have a gap in my schedule but I'm hitting my monthly financial goals, use the free time to troll for bigger, better journalism gigs and work on aforementioned essays.

If you're an illustrator or interior designer who just fled the cube last year, your biggest goal might be boosting the amount of bacon you're bringing home. (We'll get to the *how* of making moola in Part 2.) If you're an event planner or e-commerce programmer on her third year of full-time freelancing, you might be more concerned with beefing up your green client base and phasing out any planet-busters on your roster. If you're a photographer who's spent five years making a name for herself on the wedding circuit, you might want to branch into editorial work, stock photography, or portraiture.

Just like our 9-to-5 counterparts, we freelancers should always be moving toward something, be it more money, more free time, bigger and better clients, or those dream projects that are so much fun to work on that we can't stop pinching ourselves. Operate like a reactive robot-for-hire who gobbles up every gig lobbed her way and you grow stagnant, stale. Instead, you need to give yourself a promotion every now and then. Because if you don't, who will?

I'm not saying you should aspire to be the next mommy millionaire or overnight YouTube sensation. In fact, I sincerely doubt the glass ceiling is the sole reason only 3 percent of the 10.4 million women-owned businesses in the United States pull in $1 million or more in annual revenue. (For comparison, 6 percent of male-owned businesses clear the million-dollar mark.) I'm saying that one size does not fit all self-employed people. Not all of us want to be the next big thing. Some of us just want enough cash to keep a roof over our head (and a few new pairs of shoes in the closet). And some of us just want enough downtime to devote to our creative habits or kids.

I'll leave it up to you to define—in writing—how you'll know when you've truly arrived as a creative professional for hire: four-hour work-week, six-figure income, ten employees on your payroll, twenty Fortune 500 clients in your portfolio, front page of the business section, home page of Digg, opening night at Sundance, top billing at Madison Square Garden, *New York Times* best sellers list.... It's your freelance career, so it's your call.

What's Your MO?

What if you know you want to start offering your artistic, editorial, design, managerial, programming, production, or promotional talents on a freelance basis, but you haven't the foggiest clue *what* you want to animate, illustrate, design, code, write, edit, index, produce, promote, build, budget, or sell?

That's when it's time to cozy up to your favorite search engine and start spelunking. When I finish reading an article or book by a writer who has me snorting milk out my nose, you can bet I'm on her website or blog within minutes. I want to know who else she's written for, how she landed those gigs, and if her blog offers any insight into what it's like to work with those clients. More often than not, I'm turned on to a hip new publication or freelance-writing avenue I hadn't thought to pursue.

Writers certainly don't hold a monopoly on snooping. Look at all the questions you, too, can answer by doing a morning's worth of research online: What industries and companies do other animators, auctioneers, or archivists in your neck of the woods work for? Do any of these niches pique your interest? Where do other jewelry designers, comic book artists, and felt-hat makers sell their wares—online through sites like Etsy, eBay, or BuyOlympia .com? Through their own websites? In the flesh at indie craft fairs and trunk shows? Are there any local meetups for independent handywomen, home stagers, or HR professionals you can attend? Any web communities you can join? Tell-all blogs you can read? And will any of these seasoned freelancers spill some of their trade secrets if you ply them with appetizers and drinks? (Much more on making the acquaintance of your fellow photographers, pet groomers, or Pilates instructors in Chapter 7.)

Yes, you'll probably have to dabble in projects for various industries and communities to see what work appeals most to you. But thanks to the web, you can get a running start.

Do Try This at Home: Business Plan To Go

Ready to roll up your sleeves? It's time to write your own Business Plan To Go. It can be all of a paragraph or two. All you need to do is list at least three of your freelance goals for the next year. Bonus points if you also outline your game plan—your to-do's—for reaching each one. And none of this vague "I will publish a best-selling graphic novel/pull in six figures with my catering business/win three Grammys" crud. Yes, ambition is a beautiful thing, but you still need a roadmap if you want to arrive.

Think tangible, realistic, bite-size pieces. Here's an example:

DEVELOP AND WORK ON MY IDEA
FOR A GRAPHIC NOVEL THIS YEAR.
Game plan:

❶ Put myself on a weekly illustration schedule, starting January 15. Start with thirty-minute sessions first thing in the morning on Wednesdays and Fridays, and see if I can increase the session length and/or amount by March. Aim for a rough sketch of at least one panel per session.

❷ Sign up for that cartoon-publishing class at my local media center.

❸ Read blogs by and interviews with my illustrator/cartoonist heroines to see how they got their start.

Here's another:

TRICK OUT MY LIST OF GREEN PUBLICITY CLIENTS.
Game plan:

❶ Revise online portfolio to reflect what experience I do have publicizing sustainable businesses and products.

❷ Start blogging about green businesses, products, and consumer tips to boost my street cred.

❸ Join the planning committee for my local home improvement and garden show to get my name out there.

❹ Print up new business cards and introduce myself to all the green businesses in town.

Give each item in your plan a start date and a deadline. Break down the steps into bite-size pieces you can tackle each month, week, or day, and give them deadlines too. Set up whatever reward system you need to prod yourself along (vino! cupcakes! John Cusack movie night!). If you can't wrap your brain around anything beyond the next ninety days, write a three-month plan and rinse and repeat at the end of the quarter. (If you're brand-new to freelancing, consider reading Chapters 2 through 10 before taking a stab at this exercise.)

Make a spreadsheet, a wall chart, or a 3D diorama to track your progress. Take a page from Molly Crabapple and get your friends in on the act: "For big, long-term goals, I've found loudly bragging about what I'm going to do makes me do it," says the award-winning illustrator for such fine institutions as Marvel comics, *The New York Times*, and *Playgirl*. "Otherwise, I have to face the humiliation of public failure." (Talk about incentive.)

Bottom line: You're a smart kid. So if you don't have a plan about how you're going to meet this so-called freelance life head-on, time to get cracking.

Chapter 2

Forget Fuzzy Math

Get real with your finances—and get over the notion that artists have to starve

"Making money is art and working is art and good business is the best art."

—Andy Warhol

A couple years ago I attended a business conference for writers and visual artists. One of the main panels was on how to blend creativity and commerce without winding up on your office floor in the fetal position, a shell of the woman you were before you served your soul on a silver platter to the Man. After forty-five minutes of hearing half a dozen painters and illustrators elaborate on how it's next to impossible for an emerging artist to cobble together a living on watercolors and lithographs alone (no way!), someone in the audience asked what each of the panelists did for fallback income. One up-and-comer on the panel copped the "I am an Artiste!" attitude that drives me nuts. It goes something like this: "I don't have a fallback. Having a fallback is like falling down, or admitting defeat. It's like giving up on my artistic ambitions altogether. I might as well just trade in my easel now if I'm going to fall back."

So basically this Vincent Van Schmo would rather sell his paintings at the farmers market and eat Saltines for dinner than taint his Talent with any lowly commercial work.

Yeah right. And I'm the queen of Sheba.

The Beauty of Bread-and-Butter Work

If you've read *The Anti 9-to-5 Guide: Practical Career Advice for Women Who Think Outside the Cube,* my book on alt career paths, you know that although I'm a big fan of following your creative bliss, I'm also a big fan of fallback skills, backup plans, and bread-and-butter work that keeps you clothed, fed, and warm at night. I mean, what's so noble about starving? Where's the honor in sleeping on a subway grate?

Nobility, to me, is using your creative talents to invent a job for yourself and getting paid a decent wage to do it. It's taking on corporate, commercial, or commissioned work so you don't have to stress about pursuing the creative projects that thrill you most but (perhaps initially) pay the least. Maybe your master plan is to one day support yourself with your dazzling jewelry and silk-screened T-shirt line. In the meantime, there's nothing wrong with applying your artist's eye to some money-in-the-bank work designing blogs, brochures, and wedding invitations so you can feed both yourself and your creative sideline.

Besides, taking on bread-and-butter work gives you structure, which we procrastinating creative types desperately need. It gives you a chance to beef up your marketable skills (in this fickle employment market, you can't have too many). And it gives you validation in your decision to go solo, not to mention a bone to throw those family members still lamenting that you quit your day job to walk dogs, caulk bathrooms, or hawk vibrators.

More often than not, your breadwinning work will help fuel your enthusiasm for the screenplay, crocheted handbags, or life-size ceramic replica of Margaret Cho you're chipping away at on the side. The less time you have for your creative projects, the more you can't wait to return to them. Absence makes the heart grow fonder and all that.

For many, the breadwinning work leads to ideas for the creative work. Take Summer Pierre, an illustrator/musician from New York, whose part-time administrative assistant job prompted her to create *The Artist in the Office,* the inspiring zine she sells on SummerPierre.com. Or independent accounting professional Holly Bohn, from Newbury Park, California, whose frustration over the lack of attractive office supplies on the market led her to launch SeeJaneWork.com, a wildly success-ful retail and wholesale company that sells sassy office accoutrements for women. Or New York author and *BUST* magazine columnist Ayun Halliday, whose hilarious book *Job Hopper: The Checkered Career of a Down-Market Dilettante* dishes about her former odd-job days. Or the infinite number of country songs about bosses gone bad.

There are those who think that freelancing is a quaint little hobby for kept women (and men) who want to do quaint little projects a few hours a month, rather than a viable career path that can support a wom-an with a mortgage of her own, let alone an entire family of five. But I'm here to tell you those killjoys are dead wrong.

Over the years, I've met and interviewed countless females—some of them single mothers, some the sole breadwinner in a two-adult, multi-kid household—who pull in an impressive income by working for themselves full-time. There's Erin Blaskie, a virtual assistant from Ontario, Canada, who started her business at age twenty-one and was making six figures by age twenty-three. There's paper-cut artist Nikki McClure from Olympia, Washington, who feeds her family of three with the proceeds from her popular artwork, calendars, and books. There's single mother Elizabeth Mance, who started her Seattle-based boutique accounting firm in 1997 and has since hired eight employees (not to mention put her son through college). There's Alisa Geller, a personal trainer in Denver, who bought a home of her own while living single and working solo. There's Sherri Schultz, a San Francisco–based editor with fifteen years in the freelance trenches, who doubles as caregiver for her elderly aunt and her father. And on and on.

Freelancing is a job, a business, just like any other. It doesn't mat-ter how much you enjoy painting murals, playing in nightclubs, or put-ting on charity auctions. You still have to take your business as seriously as the CEO of any multimillion-dollar start-up would. Hold on to your creative, artistic ideals, yes, but don't let them rule your wallet entirely. Unless you don't mind living on rice cakes and that vague hope that Oprah will, miraculously, stumble upon your chapbook, eBay store, or YouTube video and give you a call.

What's My (Bottom) Line?

I know you're probably anxious to get to the good stuff—how to find clients, how to negotiate a contract, how to work from home without winding up like Tom Hanks in *Cast Away*, talking to a volleyball. But none of that does you any good if you don't have your bottom line in mind.

As the CEO of your own freelance venture, your first order of business, if you haven't done so already, is to figure out how much you need to earn—as in, how much you need to live on for the next year. If you've never committed a personal budget to paper, it's moment-of-truth time. Track each bagel and beer you buy for a month to see where all your dough goes, then multiply by twelve to get a tally of your annual spending. Don't forget any one-time expenses you'll have for the year, like vacations, car registration, and holiday gifts. Because until you get real with how much you need to live on, you can't accurately determine what to charge for your freelance projects and how much you'll need to work each week in order to make enough green to survive.

One of the downsides of quitting your 9-to-5 is forfeiting that free or employer-subsidized health insurance. We'll talk about options for buying your own health insurance in Chapter 15, but in the meantime, you can price plans on eHealthInsurance.com to get a rough number to plug in to your budget.

Don't worry about the costs of running your business just yet; we'll get to business expenses in Chapter 6. For now, stick to your personal expenses: rent or mortgage, food, health insurance, credit card bills, retirement savings, childcare, et cetera. If you like things automated, you can find personal budget calculators on sites like Bankrate.com and Kiplinger.com, or you can buy yourself a copy of Quicken.

If you have a lot of fat in your budget, now would be a fine time to trim it. New cocktail dress you'll wear once every three years, or quitting your job a month sooner? Two-bedroom Park Slope apartment, or ditching your day gig sometime this decade? It's your choice. I'm not saying you need to sell all your worldly possessions and live out of a van, but a little frugality never hurt anyone. Besides, if you want to live without a steady paycheck, controlling the urge to splurge is pretty much required.

On the flip side, when you work for yourself some of your personal expenses will shrink. Leave the corporate campus behind and you're likely to save a mint in commuting costs: gas, tolls, parking, car maintenance, public transport. Shocking though it may be, I've owned the same car for almost twenty years. Since I've rarely commuted to a traditional office in it, the mileage is crazy low, the upkeep is almost nil, and I get some nice car insurance discounts. But it's not just transportation costs you stand to save: Think of all the officewear, dry-cleaning bills, and $15 lunches on the run you'll no longer be paying for.

If your debt collectors have you on speed dial, now's not the time to leave the cube farm for freelance pastures. Pay down that nasty balance first. If you need help managing your debts, check out a nonprofit debt consolidation service like MoneyManagement.org. And if you need to make any big business purchases before you can freelance—say, if you're a masseuse without a massage table—do so while you still have a steady paycheck to draw from.

Many of the freelancers whose career paths I admire most—some of whom you'll meet in this book—aren't shy about facing the financial realities of self-employment head-on. They plan for and tighten their belts during the lean times. They pay their bills off and refrain from buying half of H&M's spring collection when they're flush with cash. They balance bread-and-butter work with the dream-come-true creative work as needed. And they're the first to admit that fuzzy math and artsy-fartsy ideals don't pay the bills.

As it would turn out, my self-employed heroines and I aren't the only ones who realize that it takes a healthy dose of flexibility and practicality to make a go at this crazy little thing called freelancing. Remember Vincent Van Schmo, who wouldn't dream of degrading himself with a fallback income, not even if he were living under a freeway? Five minutes further into the panel, he admitted to the ballroom of hopeful creative professionals that he actually had seven little part-time jobs he relied on to make ends meet. Not one. Not two. Seven. (I rest my case.)

Fear and Loathing of Lost Wages (a.k.a., How to Know When It's Time to Go)

Unless you have half a year's living expenses stashed under the mattress or plan to live in Mom and Dad's basement awhile, I strongly recommend wading into freelancing and keeping a part-time, temp, or otherwise flexible day job while you gather up as many contacts, clients, and portfolio pieces as you can. Take advantage of the fact that you're collecting a steady paycheck and stockpile the green, too, so that when you do touch down as a full-time freelancer, it's a soft landing. Because in case no one's enlightened you yet, for your first year in business, your income may be a bit on the skimpy side.

My first year as a freelancer, my profit amounted to a whopping $6,000. Granted, that was in the early nineties, before the web made looking for work ten thousand times easier, and back when I had the business sense (and living expenses) of a tapeworm. But still, not exactly a windfall.

To fill in the gaps, I became the queen of odd jobs. Thanks to an employment center at the local community college, I was able to drudge up scores of stopgap work handling rich people's bills, phone messages, laundry, childcare, and workshop registration (because in Marin County, California, you're nothing if you don't teach some spiritual enlightenment workshop or other). But I don't hold a monopoly in the supplemental odd job department. Seattle-based graphic artist, cartoonist, and author Ellen Forney worked the night shift on a psych ward during her first couple of years as a freelancer. Novelist and *Los Angeles Times* columnist Meghan Daum wrote everything from press releases for a state-funded mental health organization to web copy for Always Maxi Pads during her early freelance years. Molly Crabapple initially supplemented her fledgling freelance illustration business by working as a nude model for artists and photographers on the side.

freelance **tip**

Trading in your 9-to-5 for a more flexible day gig that gives you mornings, Fridays, or any other window of time off during regular business hours can make getting your freelancing business off the ground infinitely easier. Otherwise, you'll have to wake with the roosters or burn the midnight oil (and likely invest in a restaurant-grade espresso machine) to get your freelance projects done. Staying in touch with clients can be tricky too, unless you limit all communications to email, cultivate some customers in a time zone earlier than yours, or furtively sneak in a couple of calls on your cell during lunch, as I've been known to do.

How do you know when it's time to jettison your day job for good? Pick up a traditional business book and you'll probably hear that it takes a year or three before a small business owner starts pulling in enough profit to pay herself an annual salary. But as a freelancer who sells a service to companies and individuals, you won't necessarily have an avalanche of business expenses. So assuming you don't max out your credit cards buying a $7,500 computer system, and assuming you're charging your clients enough and getting paid on time, you should start seeing a profit within the first two quarters. It might not be anything to write home about, but it'll still be money in the bank.

So should you wait till your freelance income equals 30 percent of the money you need to live on before you jettison the 9-to-5 job? How about 50 percent? Or 75? And how long will all this take anyway?

There's no universal formula. "Even after I'd been published in *The New Yorker,* I still went in to temp jobs. Quite often," Meghan says.

And it took Molly, the illustrator/nude model, three years to completely phase out her modeling gigs. On the opposite end of the spectrum, Erin, the virtual assistant, nabbed her first client within two weeks of opening her doors and had enough business to quit the corporate world six months later.

In other words, it depends on how much time your day job leaves for building your freelance business, what freelance profession you're getting into, how hard you hustle, how much cash you have saved, and how much of a risk taker you are.

My motto: When freelancing on the side has you scrimping on sleep and taking caffeine intravenously, it's time to ditch the day gig. Yes, cutting the cord will be scary. Most things worthwhile in life are. But look at the bright side: When it comes to finding the extra time to grow your freelance business, you'll hit the jackpot.

Chapter 3

Get a Room Already!

Solo office smackdown: Working from home vs. putting on a pair of pants and leaving the house

"Whatever work you do at home, take every precaution to put it away properly and safely between sessions. I know of one horrible catastrophe that befell an author who had taken the only existing copy of his new novel to a typist. The dog chewed it clear through from page 100 to the end, and naturally after that the author changed typists."

—Elmer Winter, *Women at Work: Every Woman's Guide to Successful Employment*, 1961

There are many reasons not to work from home: The overflowing laundry. The blaring television. The crying kids. The rowdy roommate. The nosy neighbors. The manuscript-eating dog.

Maybe you're worried about the isolation. Or the ten trillion distractions. Or the tendency you have to fall asleep when you're within a fifty-foot radius of your bed. But in your early days as a self-employed person, unless you're a physical therapist or marriage counselor or financial planner who needs to meet with clients in a professional setting, I suggest you give working from home the ole freshman try before rushing out to rent an office.

For one thing, your home is the cheapest office space around. And as a new freelancer, one of your primary missions in life should be to keep business costs down until you know that (a) you have the financial leeway to increase your business expenses, (b) you absolutely cannot go another day without a particular business expense (such as a rented workspace), and (c) you like freelancing enough to not run back to your former boss, throw your arms around her legs, and wail, "For the love of God, please take me back!"

You might also find that you like working from home. As someone who tinkers with words for a living, I relish not having anyone else around while I'm wrestling with a paragraph that's been plaguing me for three hours. I love that I can't hear anyone else's cappuccino orders or client negotiations. I need that peace and quiet to get my work done (not to mention the freedom to dance around the house in my union suit every now and then to shake the cobwebs loose).

But it's not just me. In 2007, the U.S. Census Bureau reported that almost 4 percent of Americans work from the comfort of their own home. For some, like visual artist Nikki McClure, working at home is a necessity. She and her husband, a furniture builder who's also self-employed, take turns watching their three-and-a-half-year-old son, Finn, during the workday. Mornings, Nikki works in her backyard studio, when she's at her creative peak and "the light is best." Afternoons, she's on Finn duty. In fact, when I called her up around lunchtime midweek, Finn was in her office "playing mail" and helping her organize her tax receipts.

Before having Finn, Nikki spent eleven joyous, prolific years working at a rented studio in a downtown building bustling with other indie artists and musicians. But now that she's a mom, working at home gives her more time to actually work. "Now I can get another half hour here and there," she says. "It adds up to a couple hours a week."

People always ask how freelancers like me and Nikki pull off working from home. But it's just like riding a bike. Everyone knows how. In your 9-to-5 life, didn't you ever bring work home from the office to finish after dinner so you could meet a big deadline the next morning? Freelancing from home is no different. Finish the report for your boss, stay on her good side. Finish your work for your client, get paid. Don't finish the work in either scenario, and you get fired.

There's a halfway decent chance you'll discover you're more productive working from home than you were back in your 9-to-5 days. Remember how in your employee days, you were always getting sucked into three-hour meetings to dissect the previous day's three-hour meeting or to outline what the next day's three-hour meeting would cover? Unless your cat is extremely demanding, trust me when I say that when you work from home, this won't happen.

Mark Your Territory

Once you decide to work from home, it's critical you set up a base camp. You don't want to be a nomad, constantly in search of your pens, paints, or PDA each morning. A workspace of one's own is what you need, complete with a desk/drafting table/laptop docking station—just like you had at your 9-to-5 gig—so you can quickly dig in to each day's to-do items. (More about outfitting your office in the next chapter.)

Claim as much space as you can, preferably in a room that doesn't double as your relaxing, sleeping, or romancing quarters. Also nab yourself a workspace with a door that shuts, even locks. Alcoves, walk-in closets, spare bedrooms, or finished basements/garages are ideal.

When you're just starting out as a full-time freelancer, you may not have the luxury of abundant real estate. You may have to work in a corner of your bedroom or a sliver of your living room, as I did for many years before graduating to spare-bedroom-office status. But I like to think that if J. K. Rowling could crank out *Harry Potter and the Philosopher's Stone* in a café back in her bad old welfare mom days, freelancers like you and me can tough it out a few feet from our respective couches and TVs.

Even if you don't have an office door, you still have IKEA, Target, and countless other purveyors of beaded curtains, folding screens, and brightly colored tapestries to choose from to help separate your workspace from your off-duty space. Unless you enjoy enhanced levels of stress and feeling as though you're tethered to your laptop from dawn to dusk to dawn again, even the flimsiest of barriers will come in handy.

You also have the ability to request that any roommates, partners, children, or other family members knock or ask permission before entering your workspace, especially when you're in it.

"I live with my boyfriend now and it kind of was a transition," says writer Meghan Daum. "He didn't quite understand that my desk, which happens to be in a semi-common area of the house, is like his desk at work. I would never show up at his office and sit down in his chair. But he has no problem doing that in my chair."

The solution? Open your mouth and use it. For more about laying down the law with friends and family, see Chapter 17.

If, after six months of working alongside the wool coats and umbrellas in your hallway closet, you find yourself sketched out by your snowballing lack of hygiene, uncannily intimate friendship with your mail carrier, or encyclopedic knowledge of the guests on *The Maury Show*, you should probably consider finding yourself a workspace outside the home. (If, however, your main problem is not solitude but beating your schedule into submission, see Chapter 17.) No one would blame you; even the most reclusive freelancers get a little loopy working by their lonesome week after week.

Sometimes it's not the isolation that gets you, though, but the company. Nikki's initial incentive for renting an office was her crowded living space. "I had been living in this two-room apartment with my then boyfriend and he also made art and was self-employed," she says. "So it was like, 'Who's going to use the table?'" Hmmm—morning coin toss with your significant other over the only viable workspace in the joint. Any takers?

Your Home Office Away from Home

If you've outgrown your home office, your first thought might be to claim a space at that cute little fair trade café on the corner. However, I suggest you fight the urge to turn your neighborhood roastery into the permanent headquarters of You, Inc. Yes, your favorite coffee shop makes for a lovely three o'clock change-of-scenery break, but if you camp out there Monday through Friday, winter, spring, summer, and fall, you're bound to spend a bundle on java and baked goods you normally wouldn't consume in bulk. For the same price (or pretty darned close to it), you could rent a workspace and avoid annoying your fellow caffeine patrons with your steady stream of incoming cell calls.

In fact, you don't even have to rent your *own* office. Nor do you have to commit to renting a workspace for more than one measly day (definitely music to this commitmentphobe's ears). Coworking—renting a daily or monthly desk in a communal office of independent professionals—is well on its way to becoming the Flexcar of office setups. As I write this, independent professionals around the globe are creating and flocking to these community offices like middle managers to free donuts in the company breakroom. (See the sidebar on page 30 for more details.)

Besides being cheaper than a studio rental for one, coworking saves you from having to paint, furnish, and otherwise pimp out your workspace. In many cases, the price of admission includes coffee, wifi, landlines, photocopying privileges, and use of a conference room (no more trying to impress a potential client in Starbucks as the espresso machine roars in the background!). More important, coworking gives stir-crazy independents a place to convene, converse, and perhaps even collaborate.

"It reminds me of going to a liberal arts college and being an art major but having English majors and history majors and political science majors around me," says illustrator/animator Nina Frenkel, who rents a desk in a coworking space in New York's garment district for $450 a month. "I get inspired by stuff that's not necessarily other artists working. It feels very entrepreneurial and exciting. Everybody's desk has a different world to it. It's like, 'Oh, here's the journalist, and over here is the interior designer.' And we have a toy-inventor guy. In his workspace is a sewing machine and all this technology because he does all these high-tech plushy toys."

But companionship and creative inspiration are only part of the story, say the coworking converts. As an added bonus, it's a great way to pick up job leads. And evidently, segregating work from home does wonders for reacquainting the nose with its old friend, the grindstone. "So many people who come in are like, 'Wow that's the most productive workday I've had in a year and a half,'" says Susan Evans, an environmental consultant who cofounded Office Nomads, a five-thousand-square-foot community workspace in Seattle's Capitol Hill neighborhood.

Who knows? Maybe there is something to changing your underwear and stepping outside every morning after all.

Where the Coworkers Are

If you want to work in the company of other independent professionals, the options abound:

CREATIVE COLLECTIVES. To find a coworking office near you, see http://blog.coworking.info on the web. Rates will vary from location to location. As I write this, a monthly desk at Office Nomads in Seattle is $475 and a daily visit is $25.

STARCHED SHIRTS ONLY. If you're looking for something with a more corporate feel or need a one-time conference room, check out Regus.com or call 1-800-OFFICES for services and rates. Handy if you need an out-of-town workspace while on the road.

WRITERS' ROOMS. We word nerds like our workspaces library-quiet and dirt cheap. Fortunately, that's exactly what organizations like The Loft in Minneapolis, The Writers Room in New York, and Writers' Dojo in Portland, Oregon, offer. Check with your local arts commission or fellow scribes to see if there's one near you. (For tips on meeting your fellow freelancers, see Chapter 7.)

OLD-SCHOOL RENTALS. Perhaps you prefer a space filled with other artsy, entrepreneurial types but in your own studio. Buildings like ActivSpace on the West Coast, OfficeOps in Brooklyn, and Northrup King Building in Minneapolis are teeming with affordable solo workspaces. For rental leads near you, consult Craigslist, ArtistHelpNetwork.com, and your fellow freelancers.

CAFÉ FREESTYLE. If cash is in short supply but you're craving human contact, try working in a public space alongside a handful of fellow freelancers

⇨

➡

once in a while. Laura Fisher, a web designer in Ann Arbor, Michigan, "micro-coworks" with four to seven other tech-minded freelancers in a café a couple mornings a week. While she doesn't do what she calls her "heavy-duty, detail-oriented design or coding" at these meetups, she uses the time to swap ideas and feedback with her freelance cohorts on projects and clients. To find a similar setup near you, see workatjelly.com.

No matter where you consider renting a daily or monthly workspace, ask what services are included (reception, parking, security, wifi, quiet area, et cetera). And be sure to test-drive the facility to see if you fit in. If you're allergic to cats, coders, or khakis, you'll want to know if the place is crawling with them before you sign on the dotted line.

Your Workplace or Mine?

Sometimes another option for leaving the house will present itself: Clients ask you to work on their turf. In my early freelance years, I often received calls from clients who needed a copy jockey to work from their office a few hours or days, proofreading legal briefs, editing advertising mock-ups, or writing high-tech marketing docs—deadline: "three days ago." I dreaded the dressing and commuting, but if I needed the work, I needed the work. And so I'd shed my pajamas, hop in my car, and suck it up.

As you can imagine, working at a client's office has its pros and cons. For me, the novelty usually wears off after a week, or the first time I'm stuck behind a six-car pileup in rush hour traffic, whichever comes first. No amount of free soda or getting paid to read *People* magazine while waiting for my next batch of mouthwash ads to edit can make up for it. When I'm right under the client's schnoz, it feels too much like I'm their bitch, back in the 9-to-5 grind all over again. Either they're giving me another twenty-seven hot potatoes they need moved to the top of the pile, or they're peering over my shoulder and asking how the thing they gave me to do five minutes ago is going. Call me a prima donna, but the "Are we there yet?" management style has never enhanced my productivity.

But perhaps you've grown weary of attempting to converse with your pet ferret and don't care about any of the above. Perhaps you're thrilled to shower, leave the house, commune with other bipeds before noon, and get paid to do so. Or perhaps, like a freelancer I'll call Betty, who's been producing corporate videos for high-tech Goliaths for more than a decade, your work is far easier to conduct on the client's turf.

So what can you expect? On the upside, sitting an iPhone's-throw away from the key players on a project—in Betty's case, the people she plans budgets and production schedules with—makes your job infinitely easier. Working onsite means Betty can access her clients' internal websites, use their equipment, and learn her way around what she calls "all that infrastructure stuff" (the corporate-speak, the branding guidelines, the company culture) in a fraction of the time working from home would take.

On the downside, if you stick around long enough, you might accidentally catch a whiff of some nasty office politics. "Even if it's not your own, the office morale seeps into your life," Betty says, before launching into a scenario she had the misfortune of stepping into:

"A few years back, an office where I was working had to lay off about fifteen people and they took a year to decide which fifteen. Theoretically, it didn't affect me or the work I was doing. And I wasn't doing the job of anybody who was going to be laid off. But it was a sour place to be. I had to work with employees who were wondering if they were going to be axed, so they weren't always doing their best work. And it makes you feel like you're not quite a freelancer because you get sucked further into the corporation than you'd like to be."

Moral of the story: The grass may always be greener, but the Berber carpeting is always grayer too.

Chapter 4

Act Like a Professional

From licenses to lawyers: What you need to hang your shingle—and what you can live without

"I'm experienced now, professional. Jaw's been broke, been knocked down a couple of times, I'm bad! Been chopping trees. I done something new for this fight. I done wrestled with an alligator. That's right. I have wrestled with an alligator. I done tussled with a whale. I done handcuffed lightning, thrown thunder in jail. That's bad! Only last week I murdered a rock, injured a stone, hospitalized a brick! I'm so mean I make medicine sick!"

—Muhammad Ali in *When We Were Kings*, 1996

I remember the first time I walked into an Office Depot back in the early nineties. I'd just started working for myself as a freelance writer/editor/proofreader/publicist/typist/anything else remotely related to publishing and had not a spring but a full-blown bounce in my step. If they'd been handing out HELLO, MY NAME IS . . . tags at the door, I gladly would have filled one with thick, bubbly letters reading A FULL-TIME FREELANCER! and worn it proudly over my breast.

Here was the biggest office supply closet I'd ever seen, and it was all for freelancers and small business owners like me! No matter that nothing in the store was free. I was a professional, dammit, just like Muhammad Ali. This was my championship prizefight, and I intended to go home with as many trophies as my double-wide shopping cart would hold.

I don't remember how much that day's bloated spending spree wound up costing me in credit card interest payments, but I do remember filling several rows of kitchen cupboards with pens, pencils, erasers, highlighters, rulers, protractors, pencil sharpeners, three-hole punchers, notepads, sketchpads, paperclips, staples, rubber bands, Scotch tape, printer paper, fax paper, manila folders, bubble mailers, mailing labels, neon green photocopy paper, and what appeared to be a lifetime's supply of Post-its. While the Post-its were a surprisingly good call—I managed to use them all before the decade was out—I haven't had to buy another notepad, paperclip, or staple since.

Like me, you might be tempted to slap on a HELLO, MY NAME IS FREDA FREELANCE! name tag, grab your wallet, and outfit yourself to the gills: $500 espresso machine, $1,500 Aeron chair, $15,000 garage-to-office conversion. Don't. Trust me, eventually the debt catches up with you, and it will suck. Hard. (If you don't believe me, see "Debit or Credit?" in Chapter 15.)

Then again, there's being frugal, and there's pinching your pennies so tight you get calluses. Yes, in the interest of testing the freelance waters, you should only pour your time, money, and energy into the equipment and services you absolutely need. But don't go so bare-bones your business gets KO'd in the first round.

The Necessary Accoutrements

As we've already established, when I was starting out as a freelancer, I was a little confused as to which went first—the cart or the horse. Save for buying a lifetime's supply of paper clips, I blazed right past all that snoozy infrastructure stuff and took a flying leap—cannonball style—into the deep end of the freelance pool. Unfortunately, this hastiness wound up costing me time and money I couldn't really spare (in other words, lots of eleventh-hour rush fees). If I could hit rewind and start over again, I'd definitely take a couple weeks to set my business up properly.

Don't let this scare you. Setting up shop is far less daunting than it sounds, and nowhere near as costly. In fact, once you've figured out where you'll work, hanging your freelance shingle doesn't require much overhead at all. Herewith, my start-up shortlist of what you need to do, buy, barter, scavenge, and organize right away:

FILL YOUR TOOLBOX. Populate your home office with any electronics, software, supplies, furniture, and storage items you expect to use at least once a week—computer peripherals, dedicated business phone, dedicated email account (preferably not JuicyJD@hotmail.com or CurvyCPA@gmail.com), headset, printer/fax/scanner/copier, whiteboard, file cabinet, bookshelves, et cetera. Before you buy new, look to eBay, Craigslist, and clearance sales. And if you're not sure you'll use that digital recorder, light meter, or guitar amp more than a couple times a year, hold off on buying it; borrow it instead, or split the cost with a couple other freelance friends in need.

MAKE A (DIGITAL) DISASTER PLAN. You of course need a trusty computer that doesn't conk out every time you're on deadline and a zippy Internet connection that you don't have to pirate from your neighbors down the street. And just like Cagney and Lacey, you need backup. Emailing the file you're working on to your Gmail account for safekeeping is a sloppy way to go; better to get an external hard drive or storage system that can hold every save-worthy file on your computer, which, whether you like it or not, has been programmed to die while you're working on the most important and financially lucrative project of your life.

I have a nifty little flash drive that holds 250 gigabytes, plugs into a USB port at the back of my laptop, and is about the size of my hand. In 2008, it cost $250, including the spiffy carrying case. By the time you read this, it will likely be grossly outdated, replaced with some smaller, cheaper, more reliable backup product with one hundred times the memory. To choose a backup system of your own, decide how much memory you need, how small you want the drive to be, and how much you're willing to spend. For product reviews, see CNET.com; for user reviews, see Newegg.com or Amazon.com. Then get the best bargain you can find. If, like me, you're an utter Luddite, enlist the help of a gadget-loving pal.

Rather than wait for your computer to self-destruct, create your contingency plan now. Will you ring up Geek Squad for a house call? Or will you apply pressure, stop the bleeding, and race your gasping laptop to the nearest repair shop? While your laptop's convalescing, what will you work on? That spare clunker you keep in the closet? A freebie CPU at the library? Don't be the frazzled freelancer trying to pry her five-year-old hardcopy of the Yellow Pages out from under her spluttering monitor when the digital shit hits the fan.

GO ERGO. This probably won't seem important when you're hunched over your laptop on your mushy living room couch, tickled that you're actually getting paid to work from your mushy living room couch. Three months later when you're crying to your chiropractor about lower back pain, you'll think differently. Get yourself a good ergonomic chair with lumbar support, a desk that's the right height, a footrest, an ergo keyboard, and any other accessories you need to stave off back and wrist pain. As you'll see in Chapter 16, it's all a tax write-off.

NAME THE BABY. Birth name, pseudonym, or business name? The choice is yours. Personally, I'm a fan of using the name my mama gave me. Then again, that's pretty much the way of the journalism and book-writing world. When in doubt, look to your industry for cues. If you're a stand-up comic or stand-up bass player, you'll probably want to use your own name or a stage name. "I started using a pseudonym when I was nude modeling," says illustrator Molly Crabapple (born Jennifer Caban). "It's the standard practice. Since I starting making art professionally at the same time, it seemed a shame to waste the fan base."

On the other hand, if you're a Feldenkrais practitioner, e-commerce programmer, or concert promoter, you'll want to think up a catchy name so customers know you mean business. (Bonus points for creativity.) Steer clear of "cutesy" spellings like Koder's Korner, which scream strip mall. Ditto for adding a trademark symbol (TM) to your business name (and every other line on your website and marketing materials), which smacks of infomercial.

If you do go with a business name (what's known as a DBA, "doing business as," or fictitious business name), sites like MyCorporation .com and LegalZoom.com make registering it a snap, something you need to do for tax, banking, and legal purposes. Or you can do it the old-fashioned (and cheaper) way, through your county clerk's office. Usually this involves filling out an innocuous form, paying a nominal fee, and sometimes, publishing a notice in your local newspaper. Note: If you plan to use your legal name as part of your business name (for example, Michelle Goodman Musings), you still may need to register a DBA, depending on the laws in your state. To learn more about registering your business name in your state, see business.gov/guides/business_law /dba.html.

Before you commit your chosen name to paper, ask ten people you trust for their honest opinion. Then Google it to make sure it's not already being used by another enterprising free-lancer in another state.

GET LEGIT. For new freelancers, "How much do I have to make before I need a business license?" seems to be the $64,000 question. The IRS defines "business" as any activity you embark on that makes a profit; otherwise, you're considered a hobbyist. Cities and states like to follow the IRS's lead (more tax dollars for them!). For that reason, the second you start earning any business income, they want you to register for a business license. Even if you're doing business under your own name (as opposed to a company name), you have to get the license. Licensing requirements vary by city, state, and industry but usually aren't too spendy; a quick visit to your city or state department of licensing website can give you the scoop. To learn more about business licensing in your state, see sba.gov/hotlist/license.html.

Like many freelancers, I put off getting a business license for a few years. The whole thing sounded so intimidating. Then I landed a cash cow client that required me to have a state business license. So I bit the bullet—and soon found myself wondering what I had been so afraid of. All that was involved was filling out a simple form through my state's department of licensing website and paying $15. That was ten years ago, and I haven't had to renew the license since. Figuring that my city would eventually catch wind of my state business license and come after me, I got myself a city business license too. While filling out the online form was a snap, the City of Seattle business license fee was a bit steeper—about $100 annually. (Again, the rates and rules will vary widely depending where you live and what you do for a living.)

freelance tip

If you plan to conduct business with clients in your home or plan to hire employees to work from your home office, make sure that you're not violating any pesky residential zoning laws, or that you don't need any additional business permits. Again, the rules will vary from business to business and location to location; check with your city, state, or county government for details. If you're just planning to write marketing copy or design web pages in your living room all by your lonesome, chances are none of these rules and regs will affect you. (In all the years I've been working from home, they've never affected me.) It's generally when your business starts generating a lot of foot traffic or creating a lot of noise that this could become a problem for you—since that's when the neighbors might decide to file a complaint.

What does your business license get you? A nice certificate for your bulletin board (actually quite exciting at first blush), the right to pay city and/or state taxes (often you get a break during the early, lean years), the seal of approval from any business banking services or corporate clients that require you to have a business license number, and a bunch of junk mail.

I know what you're thinking: *But I just started freelancing . . . so do I really need a business license?* According to the rules, yes. Whether your regional government finds out that you're only grossing $25,000 your first year in business is anyone's guess. But whether you want to risk it (and any potential penalties) is your call.

BE A CARD-CARRYING FREELANCER. You wouldn't leave home without condoms, right? So too with business cards. You never know when you might get lucky and meet the freelance lead of your dreams. Thanks to sites like MOO.com, 48HourPrint.com, OvernightPrints.com, and VistaPrint.com, making sassy business cards is cheap and easy.

Don't be afraid to make your cards offbeat, funny, outrageous. Remember, you're trying to showcase your *creativity*. My writer pal Diane Mapes has a retro-looking waitress holding a pot of coffee on her card, which inquires, CAN I GET YOU ANOTHER CUP OF COPY? And recently I saw an amazing card on a blog that was essentially a mini envelope stuffed with alfalfa seeds that grow (out of the card!) when placed in water. The tagline? ANOTHER BLOOMIN' DESIGNER. What client could resist that brilliance?

Call me paranoid, but I won't put my street address on my business cards. Instead, I rent a PO box and use that addy. (Helps keep my checks and tax forms safe, too.) Unless you run a business where clients visit your office regularly, you might as well keep the whereabouts of your private residence, well, private.

CALL DIRK IN ACCOUNTING. If you think you don't need to worry about paying your taxes till early in the calendar year, think again. This may come as a shock to some of you, but freelancers don't get taxes taken out of their checks. Instead, self-employed folks send their taxes directly to Uncle Sam—in quarterly installments, no less.

So the sooner you get yourself a good accountant and set up an accounting system for yourself, the better (help on the way in Chapter 16). You don't want to realize on April 1 that you have no idea how much money you made the previous year, you didn't track your business expenses (let alone make your quarterly payments), and you have no clue how to do your taxes.

I pay my CPA $350 dollars a year to prepare my tax returns, which, as far as I'm concerned, is a small price to pay to keep the government out of my hair. To find a good accountant near you, turn to your fellow freelancers for referrals. (More on how to meet other freelancers in Chapter 7.) It doesn't matter whether you hire an accountant or a CPA (which is a fancy way of saying "accountant who's taken a pile of certification exams"). The most important thing is to hire a tax professional who predominantly works with small businesses and freelancers—preferably freelancers doing the same type of work as you—so she's familiar with the type of expenses and issues your business might have.

Stop the Presses

Yet another thing I wasted hundreds of dollars on when I first started working solo was letterhead. No logo, just "MG Communications"—a business name I abandoned after a year—with my address and phone number (also abandoned after a year, along with the boyfriend they came with). I paid a designer and everything. And a traditional printer. Of course, this was before software and the web made it a snap to fiddle with templates and create cheap letterhead yourself, but still. I thought being a professional meant having My Own Monogrammed Stationery, and so I blindly bit.

In your zeal to get this freelance party started, you too may be tempted to print up letterhead, brochures, sticky pads, postcards, mailing labels, and all manner of swag. But before you do, think about whether you'll actually have occasion to use the stuff in today's remote worker–friendly business world, or whether you'll wind up with some pricey scrap paper like I did. What professional "letters" will you be sending, and to whom? Where do you plan to distribute those glossy brochures, personalized key chains, and fridge magnets of yours?

My primary form of correspondence with clients is email, whether I'm sending a letter of introduction or an invoice. So I've done without printed stationery for more than a decade. As for brochures, if you're a masseuse

⇨

➡️

who attends the occasional mind/body trade show to try to woo new clients, the printing costs may pay for themselves in one weekend. Ditto if you know a few chiropractors, gyms, and yoga studios willing to display your trifolds at their reception desk. But if you're a virtual assistant who doesn't expect to meet 90 percent of her clients, you're better off putting your time and money into a spiffy website (conveniently, the next chapter's topic).

The one piece of swag I admit to being gaga over is the printed postcard, now affordable for mere freelancing mortals thanks to companies like 1800Postcards.com and PrintRunner.com ("Here's an easy way to remember my website—it's right on this pretty postcard!"). I love giving them away at promo events, and I love it when illustrators, photographers, and clothing designers snail mail me postcards announcing a new product or show.

Pet photographer Emily Rieman, whose clients include much of Seattle's indie rock royalty, says her $800 splurge on postcards made all the difference when she opened for business a decade ago:

"I think that made people take me a little more seriously. It was also the only advertising I had at the time and I think I was correct in assuming how to get people to remember me. People still to this day describe the card they have on the fridge, and it's one of my cards from eight years ago."

Guilty as charged. I ogle at the shot of her adorable pooch Dexter every time I pour myself a glass of orange juice.

Sole Proprietor, LLC, Inc.—WTF?

A lot people mistakenly think you need to incorporate your business in order to work as a freelancer. Maybe they believe putting letters after their business name sounds more Muhammad Ali. Or they enjoy talking to lawyers and finding additional reasons to part with their hard-earned cash. Or they're terrified to lift a pinky toe off the diving board and prefer to languish awhile in the business planning phase.

A corporation, in plain English, is a business structure that requires you to go through a bunch of legal rigmarole to set up and maintain. Think shareholder meetings, corporate record keeping, labyrinthine tax returns, and a heap of legal fees. The advantage? If your business implodes and you can't pay your professional debts, you get to keep your shirt, your dresser, and the house you store them in. A limited liability company (LLC) is more like Corporation Lite—same protection of your personal assets, only easier to run than a corporation, less of a headache at tax time, and, for reasons still not entirely clear to me, more suited for a freelance company of one.

But you'd be wise to wait till your business gets a little further along before going through the expense and trouble of forming such a legal entity. You're better off staying a sole proprietor, which, according to the law, is the type of business entity you automatically became the day you declared yourself a freelancer, no paperwork required. (As a sole proprietor, you and your business are indistinguishable in the government's eyes—you share the same tax return, and if your business has debts, so do you.)

Before you go messing with your business structure, you want to see if this freelance thing sticks, or if you desperately miss your old boss. You want to see what clients you gravitate toward, whether they require you form such a legal entity (many won't), and how vulnerable you do or don't feel having your personal assets dangling in the breeze. (Hint: If you're not worried about getting sued or reneging on your debts, you probably don't need to up the business-entity ante.) Besides, at several hundred dollars an hour, you may want to stave off consulting with a legal professional for as long as humanly possible.

I have worked with a couple of Fortune 500 clients that would only outsource to freelancers who'd formed a corporation or an LLC. Because I decided to move my business in another direction (less corporate work, more journalism and creative writing), I decided to skip the fancy legal structure. I've still had the opportunity to work with those Fortune 500s, but I've done so through a creative agency (often a business of one who decided to incorporate)—in other words, by getting hired as a subcontractor. Don't worry, though, we'll talk about this kind of work in Chapter 7.

If you have a lot of personal assets (house, savings, Heavyweight Boxing Championship belt) and you work in a highly competitive,

volatile industry (web, high-tech, the insurance industry itself), professional liability insurance can't hurt (different from personal liability
insurance). Not only can it help protect you from a lawsuit-happy client, it's often cheaper and easier than forming an LLC. We'll talk about
insurance a bit more in Chapter 15. Meanwhile, if you're dying to cram
your brain with additional details about corporate structures, see Nolo.
com, a fantastic clearinghouse of free legal information that even your
dog can understand.

So that's it, killer. Tackle the to-do's covered in this chapter (and
back-burner the bells and whistles you don't need right away), and
you'll be in business—literally.

Okay, who's ready to step in that ring and wrestle some alligators?

Chapter 5

Put Your Best Bunny-Slippered Foot Forward

Why you absolutely, unequivocally need a web portfolio and how to make one

"What we need is a nationwide network of information superhighways, linking scientists, business people, educators, and students by fiber-optic cable."

—Al Gore, *The Futurist*, 1991

I love the web, and not just because it's the best place to find photos of half-bald, half-sober celebrities prone to wardrobe malfunctions. I love the web because it's the best place I know for enticing new clients without even having to lace my shoes.

It doesn't matter if you've been working for yourself one day or one decade, or if you have an annual budget of $100 or $100,000. Join the online party and there's always a place for you at the table, right alongside all those start-up billionaires, best-selling authors, oft-quoted artists, Etsy Showcasers, eBay PowerSellers, Top 100 bloggers, most-viewed YouTubers, and anyone else who's slept, clawed, or bootstrapped their way into the public eye.

I know you don't need me to convince you that getting yourself a website (or updating the one you haven't changed since 2003) is good for business. You know it makes your business look more hip, happening, and, well, businesslike. You know it makes it infinitely easier for people three time zones away to find you, sneak a peek at your work, and discover how hard you rock before even calling to see what your availability is. You know it's the de facto standard for freelancers who want their phone to ring.

But have you considered how much time and energy having a web portfolio could save you? New York documentary filmmaker/cinematographer Hope Hall explains it this way:

"In negotiating new jobs, I used to spend a lot of time talking on the phone, giving the same speech when asked to describe my work and my approach. We would then move to the 'Why don't you come by with some of your work?' or the 'Send me your reel' part of the conversation, and I would feel exhausted. We weren't even negotiating the terms yet, and I would have spent what felt like hours on this job already. My website changed the whole process of negotiating possible jobs. I just refer people to it and then say that if there is a specific piece that makes sense for them to see all the way through, I'll be happy to get that to them. It is a basic website, only three pages, with a resume, a bio, and a filmography that links to excerpts or whole pieces, but I constructed it with words and images that reflect something a phone conversation (or an email) cannot."

Long story short: Time is money, especially when you can't bill for all those "getting to know me" phone calls. So why waste it repeating the same old spiel over and over?

I know that you're busy. And that if you're not a web designer, you may be unsure where to start, and possibly prone to involuntary eye twitches upon hearing terms like "content management system" and "search engine optimization." I was all those things before I launched my first website in 2006. I still am. But that's not gonna stop me from working the web anyway—not when the web is the most likely place for potential customers to find me. Nor should it stop you.

Anatomy of a Digital Portfolio

You don't need a $5,000 graphically designed corporate logo to be admitted to the digital party. Nor, as Hope just attested, do you need a fifteen-page, text-heavy, image-riddled site crammed with more data than the *Encyclopaedia Britannica*. Think of your site as your digital portfolio or brochure: clean, streamlined, easy to read.

"I'm of the opinion that less is more," says Emily Carlin of Jacksonville, Florida, cofounder of Swank Web Style, a seven-woman virtual design studio catering to freelancers, bloggers, and small business owners. "For a portfolio, limiting yourself to one to four pages is your best bet. People are inherently lazy, and you don't want to bombard them with a million pages/paragraphs of text (they *aren't* going to read it) or confuse them with links all over the place (they won't bother clicking on all of them). I say let your work speak for itself."

So, where to start? Before you think about whether you'll create your website yourself, bribe a technically inclined pal to help, or cough up several hundred to a couple thousand bucks for a professional web designer (more on this shortly), you need to figure out what you want to put on your site and get a rough idea of how you'd like it to look.

Your first stop should be the online homes of your creative idols and competitors. What do you love about their sites? Hate? How can you make yours stronger, better, fantastic-er? As with business cards, don't be afraid to be unique and inventive. Isn't that what your clients are paying you for?

One of my all-time favorite websites is NoOneBelongsHereMore ThanYou.com, the promo site for filmmaker/performing artist/writer Miranda July's first book of short stories. It's hilarious, brilliant, and crazy-original. If there were any rules of website making, this site would probably violate them all. That's what I love most about it.

The last thing the world needs is another bland portfolio site sporting nonsensical corporate-speak and generic images of suited execs with their arms folded over their chests. Unless you're trying to woo angel investors or clients like Donald Trump, why pretend you're a bigger gun (and a bigger stick in the mud) than you are? Clients tired of working with uninspired, overpriced, bureaucratic firms will see your "boutiqueness" as an asset, so you might as well milk it.

Wendy Merrill, who founded WAM Marketing Group, a virtual agency of freelancers serving the biomed industry, certainly does. Her website, WAMGroup.net, talks about her Northern California–based company's "brash new take on the familiar agency model" and "agency-quality work—*without* agency overhead." I suspect I'm not the only one who's visited it and thought, *Amen.*

That said, you do want to be mindful of your audience. If you're targeting straitlaced law and accounting firms, a site peppered with overly whimsical, psychedelic graphics could miss the mark. When in doubt, play it safe. The beauty of a website is that you can always change it later as your business and client base grows.

So what are the staples of the freelancer's digital portfolio, aside from your all-important contact information?

YOUR BIO. While there's no one-size-fits-all formula, you can't go wrong with two or three carefully crafted paragraphs that sum up your career highlights—how many years you worked as a creative lead at Google before going solo, that All My Competitors Are Dying with Envy award you just received, and so on. Again, the sites of your freelance heroes can be a big source of ideas and guidance here.

Depending on your profession and industry, potential clients may want to see a full-blown resume rather than just a three- or four-paragraph bio. I usually need to show a resume to my copywriting and journalism clients. Likewise, many filmmakers, designers, editors, software testers, project managers, and college instructors I know are asked to do the same. Again, look to the websites of other freelancers in your profession for clues about whether a resume is the norm (many freelancers have both a bio and a resume on their site), as well as what details to include. When it comes to crafting a freelance resume, almost anything goes, as long as the content is clear, concise, professional, and no longer than a couple pages.

Give people a sense of who you are, and include a photo if you want, but steer clear of TMI (too much information) territory. "I don't need to know the names of your pets, but I might want to hear why you do this work and what it means to you," says Karrie Kohlhaas, owner of ThoughtShot Consulting in Seattle, which helps independent professionals market and grow their businesses. "Knowing you have two cats, a hamster, and a ferret just makes me think your house smells, but hearing that you have been collecting iconic images since age five makes me think, 'This person has spent a lifetime preparing for a career to help me with my logo.'"

YOUR WORK SAMPLES. Easy to find, easy to open is my motto. No one wants to slog through a bunch of broken links, Flash animations (unless you're trolling for animation work), or PDF downloads. "Your work should be the most important thing on the page, not some flashing graphic or annoying music (that no one wants to hear, by the way)," says Emily of Swank Web Style. "If they have to wait too long or if it doesn't work, they're just going to give up and never come back."

While I'm all for saving trees, I'm not advocating we write off print and otherwise tactile portfolios just yet. Even if you meet with potential clients but once a year, you still need to show up armed with your bio (or resume), press kit, headshot, laptop, slide show, print ads, product samples, color samples, demos, illustrations, animations, or publications. No matter what tactile tools you use to show off your talents, keep them dusted, cued up, and at the ready, just in case you get that call you've been waiting for all year.

If you're not sure you can use a sample on your site—perhaps because you don't own the license, or the information is proprietary—check with your client. Better to be safe than a contract violator. And if you don't have any work samples yet, Part 2 can help. Meanwhile, you may want to put the brakes on building your website.

Protect Your Work from Digital Thieves

Unfortunately, the web makes it easier for shady freelance wannabes to steal the work of others and try to pass it off as their own. But the good news is that there are many ways you can protect your blog posts, articles, artwork, images, and ideas from these online bandits.

Even though you own the copyright to your work the moment you create it, registering it with the Library of Congress gives you additional legal recourse against thieves. To learn how to register any content you create, see the U.S. Copyright Office at Copyright.gov.

Regardless of whether you register your work, add the following line to each page of your website to deter thieves: "Copyright © [year site was created] – [current year] by [your name or company name]. All rights reserved." Alternatively, you can choose to share some rights to your work under what's called a Creative Commons license (say, if you want to let people repost articles from your blog on their own site, as long as they attribute your work to you and link back to your site). For more info, see CreativeCommons.org.

To further protect illustrations, photography, and other visual work from thieves, only use low-resolution images on your site, which makes them worthless to those who might steal them for stock photography or print use. Or use a freeware program like Pictureshark, which lets you create a watermark over each image. To protect your written text from plagiarists, set Google alerts (which automatically search on any words you specify) and use tools like Copyscape to see if anyone's been stealing your content.

For dozens of other copyright tips, see the article "Take it Back! 100 Tips to Defeat Content Thieves" on VirtualHosting.com/blog (to find it, search on "copyright"). If someone does steal your content, send them a civilized note (no need to get nasty right away) insisting they remove your work from their website. If they ignore or refuse you, contact their web hosting service to explain the situation and request that the web hosting company shut down the thief's site.

YOUR CLIENT LIST. Besides impressing new customers by dropping the names of your hotshot clients, you may want to include some of your rave reviews. ("Not only does Michelle deliver dazzling prose, she and her mean guacamole are a welcome addition at our annual picnic.") Prospective customers will naturally want to know what others think of your work (and perhaps your bean dip). Why not make it easy for them?

FREQUENTLY ASKED QUESTIONS. If you find yourself repeatedly answering the same questions ("No, I don't photograph boa constrictors, only puppies and kittens"), a How I Work, Services Offered, or FAQ page could save you some time and migraines. The one thing I would leave off your site, though, is your rate. If your projects vary in size, complexity, and industry, you don't want to box yourself in with a project or hourly rate that may not apply universally. (More on pricing in the next chapter.) There are some exceptions of course, say if you work as a pet sitter, portrait photographer, or psychologist, fields where giving the hourly or session rate is common.

Siteomatic: Website Design Made Simple

Okay, let's dive right into the site making. Here's what you'll need:

A DOMAIN NAME. I suggest you purchase your own domain name (for instance, MySuperImpressiveWebsite.com). It will cost you all of ten bucks a year, if that. More important, it's much more pro and much easier for clients to find and remember than a web address like this: SomeProfessionalOrganization.com/MichelleGoodman or MichelleGoodman.SomeBloggingTool.com.

A WEB HOSTING SERVICE. If you want your own domain name, you need one of these. Ask other freelancers which web hosts they recommend. Again, this shouldn't cost you much. I pay $100 a year for mine. A good host will walk you through the domain naming process (and even give you the name for free your first year). Some web designers also offer domain name and hosting services, a boon if you prefer one-stop shopping.

A WEB DESIGNER. If I lost you at "domain name," you definitely need a web designer or a geeky pal to walk you through the process. But for a moment, let's assume I haven't lost you. Let's assume that you've been blogging for three years at MyRadFoodieBlog.Blogspot.com, know at least three HTML tags, and want to take a crack at designing your own site. There's still a decent chance this could happen: "I tried to design my own web page without much in the way of skills," says illustrator Molly Crabapple. "Bad idea. Websites are the business suits of our generation. You shouldn't settle for an ugly knockoff. For over a year, my crappy, un-updated site kept me from sending my portfolio around." (Note: Her website is gorgeous now.)

Ever frugal, I too tried to hand-make my first digital business suit. Translation: I chose a free, supposedly user-friendly web publishing tool and pestered my patient, HTML-savvy-ish boyfriend to customize the colors and header, an exercise that resulted in lots of collective swearing at the computer and me having to live with some site hiccups neither of us could fix. And while I do adore how my homegrown site looks, there are a lot of features I wish it had and things I wish it did.

But rather than spend fifty hours trying to tailor it myself (I mean, banging my head against the pixilated wall and driving my boyfriend insane), I plan to cough up the cash this year and pay a designer to make over my site the way I want—in a fraction of the time it would take me. Instead, I'll spend the time saved writing, something I actually can get paid to do, which, conveniently, will more than cover the cost of hiring the web designer.

You shouldn't have to pay a designer thousands upon thousands of dollars for a simple four-page portfolio site. Prices will of course vary, so get a few estimates if need be. If cash is extremely tight, see if you can find a baby designer at your local art school who's willing to do the deed on the cheap. As Seattle author, überblogger, and social media guru Ariel Meadow Stallings says, "You'll get a better-looking site, at way better rates, and you'll be helping a young geekling build their portfolio." And who doesn't love it when everybody wins?

Obviously you want a designer who comes recommended and whose work you like. If your "web designer" only has print samples, find someone else. You'll still have to hire a web coder to finish the job. Not ideal. Also make sure you hire a designer who's worked with freelancers who do what you do. If you're a singer/songwriter, for example, you need a designer who can get your videos, demo tracks, and audio downloads onto your site.

A WEB PUBLISHING PLATFORM. Don't be the gal with the site held hostage by the Web Guy who designs and runs. You want to be able to easily modify text, photos, and links on your site whenever you please. Having your site designed in a so-simple-a-monkey-could-edit-it content management system like WordPress or Movable Type makes this possible.

To Blog or Not to Blog?

That seems to be the question on every freelancer's tongue these days. It's definitely on mine, even though I have a blog. If I may channel my inner Tevye a moment:

Every hour I spend blogging is an hour I could have spent writing a bylined, paid article for a major media outlet, a humor essay, or a chapter of a book. On the other hand, the viral effects of a blog well done are undeniable. Each month, more and more people take a seat in your virtual living room, some of them even bearing gifts: friendship, freelance job offers, media interviews, increased sales of your product(s), news that they just told a hundred thousand of their closest online friends about your work. I certainly have my blog to thank for all of the aforementioned.

"A blog really is a great way to promote yourself, network, and get noticed," says Ariel, who blogs professionally for Microsoft, and has kept her own blog, Electrolicious.com, since 2000. In 2007, she launched the blog OffbeatBride.com, which seems to double its web traffic every time I blink and has driven up sales of her book (*Offbeat Bride*) considerably. "Granted, it's not easy work (there's nothing sadder than an abandoned blog that hasn't been updated for eighteen months), but the payoffs are remarkable. You'll show up higher in search engines, get questions and comments from people you didn't know were looking at your website, and have the opportunity to impress your prospective clients with your latest thoughts."

Ariel works on her personal blogs about twenty hours a week; I'm lucky if I spend five or six on mine. (Naturally, she has more readers.) To keep people coming back, both of us stick to our respective themes (alt weddings, alt careers), write posts several times a week, and voice our opinions liberally.

If you decide blogging isn't your cup of tea, you can still reap some of the same networking and search engine rewards through these simple additions to your website:

SHARE YOUR EXPERTISE. I love when freelancers include helpful resources and articles on their sites. Makes me want to visit their digital living room again and again, guacamole and chips in hand. Fiction writer Angela Fountas offers some excellent resources and advice for creative writers on her site, WriteHabit.org. Scotland-based web designer Rachel DuBois never seems to be out of small business website tips on DoGood-Design.com. Women's money coach Mikelann Valterra has a pile of helpful articles on boosting your income on her site, WomenEarning .com. Travel journalist Amanda Castleman has a great Travel Writing 101 page on AmandaCastleman.com. And so on.

LEARN TO LOVE KEYWORDS. Search engine goddess that she is, Ariel explained keywords to me thusly: "What would *you* search for if you were looking to hire someone like yourself? Think outside the box of your title or business. For instance, not just 'Chicago financial consultants' but 'Chicago tax advice.' Once you've picked your keywords, make sure to use them on your site—especially in the names of your pages.

MyWebsite.com/tax-advice.html is a way better name for a page than MyWebsite.com/page1.html." Got it?

MAKE A RESOURCE PAGE. That way, you can swap links with other creative types you admire. You can never have too much word of mouth or too high a search engine ranking. And blog or no, more links lead to a better Google rank. Which of course leads to more clients finding you out of the blue.

So, to sum up, class, when it comes to creating a website, personable and accessible is the new black. Trying to look like you're the next IBM? A definite website don't. "If you've got something good to say, if you've got a good product to sell, you don't need a website that looks like you spent $20,000 on it," says Colleen Lynn, owner of VainNotion, a Seattle- and Austin-based web design firm that serves start-ups. "Much better to go simpler and have that unique flair and personality."

Chapter 6

Name Your Price
Better living through solvency

"I don't get out of bed for less than $10,000 a day."

—Supermodel Linda Evangelista

B ack in my twenties when I was a freelancer-in-bloom, I briefly dated a guy who liked to call me "Little Miss Fifty Dollars an Hour." I'm pretty sure I was the first person he knew who set her own salary. To him, I was an anomaly, a puzzle, an exotic breed.

Exactly how much did I charge for those press releases I was always writing? he inquired. I tried to tight-lip it, but he kept asking. He was dashing; I relented.

"$250 each," I told him, explaining that between research, first draft, and revisions, each press release took five hours to complete. Quick on his feet, my date dubbed me "Little Miss Fifty." To his mind, I was living high on the hog, bringing home close to $500 a day, $2,500 a week, roughly $125,000 a year.

Unfortunately, he was off by a zero.

What my dashing companion failed to comprehend was that although I made $50 an hour writing press releases, I wasn't writing press releases forty hours a week; ten hours a week was more like it. As my freelance business was in its infancy, I spent most of the workweek trying to drum up new clients, doing jobs that paid far less than $50 an hour, and taking care of my invoicing, contracts, and filing. As is par for the freelance course, I wasn't billing clients for every hour I worked, unless it was an hour I worked for *them*. So on any given week, I was spending 25 to 50 percent of my time hustling for new gigs and playing office manager—work no one was paying me to do.

Another point my companion failed to grasp is that I didn't take home all of that $50 an hour I was (sporadically) making. In fact, I was lucky if my $50 hourly rate yielded $25 in my pocket. Reason being, out of each month's windfall, I'd have to take into consideration my health insurance premiums, my Office Depot and telecom bills, my retirement account contribution, and the 25 to 30 percent I'd be anticipating for city, state, and fed taxes. (More IRS fun in Chapter 16.)

Depending on whom you ask, freelancers tend to get paid about 40 to 100 percent more per hour than their employee counterparts—and I've asked a lot of people, freelancers and clients alike. There's no point in trying to adhere to some magical formula when figuring out how much more to charge as a freelancer. Instead, you need to calculate what rate will fairly compensate you.

Trust me, this isn't as painful as it sounds. I'm going to make figuring out what to charge—and ensuring you wind up in the black—easy for you. So get out your pencils and calculators, kids. It's time for first-period math.

Balance the Budget

First off, grab that personal budget I told you to make in Chapter 2. If you didn't do this yet, it's time to face the music. A key ingredient in cooking up your freelance rate is figuring out how much you need to live on each month.

Once you have your personal budget down, make a budget for your first year's business expenses—Internet access, web hosting service, craft/art/office supplies, business phone, and so on. Be sure to include any one-time purchases you'll need to get this freelance party started—an ergonomic chair and footrest, a drafting table, a computer that doesn't crash every time you turn it on. Like I said in Chapter 3, consider holding off on renting office space until you're absolutely sure you have enough business to cover the cost.

As a writer, once you take away the health insurance headache, my overhead's pretty minimal. My biggest expenses are usually the blasted cell phone bill, the blasted Internet bill, the books and magazines I buy for research, professional memberships and conferences, new computer peripherals, the occasional cross-country trip to meet with clients, and the money I pay consultants (accountant, web designer, geek for hire).

If you're a photographer, however, you need lighting equipment to get the job done. If you're a video producer, you need a PDA. If you're a financial forecaster, you might need three different number-crunching programs. If you're a musician, you probably need effects pedals, amps, and the obligatory van with flames painted on the side. If, however, you're not sure what accessories, supplies, and setup you'll need, doing some online detective work and joining a professional Listserv, networking group, or web community can go a long way.

freelance tip

To keep the best records, track your business expenses separately from your personal ones. Keeping your chocolate out of your peanut butter will make your life easier at tax time, when you'll need to add up business expenses so you can deduct them on your annual tax return. Hardly the place to muddy things up with receipts from your lost Vegas weekend.

Now let's factor in your taxes. Add up your annual personal expenses and business expenses and tack on 30 percent of the total for the annual taxes you'll owe. (Check with your accountant for the exact percentage of income you'll need to pay in taxes; more on this in Chapter 16.) So let's say it costs you $40,000 a year to live and $10,000 a year to work. The math would be $50,000 + (.30 x 50,000) = $65,000 a year. So $65,000 is the minimum amount of bacon you need to bring home each year to break even. But that's not how much—or should I say, how little—you should be earning. Read on.

Pick a Number, Any Number . . .

That's right, pick a number. But try not to get too carried away here. If you were making fifty grand as a staff project manager six months ago, it's nowhere near realistic to expect to earn $150,000 a year as an independent PM, at least not right away.

I suggest aiming for a profit at least 30 percent above your break-even point. Why? Because I can tell you from experience that (a) living month-to-month sucks, (b) you'll need a little extra money lying around should a client forget to pay up (it happens); your computer, camera, or cell phone die; or the class, conference, or retreat of your dreams come along, and (c) you'll want some mad money for personal savings/investments, trips, and miscellaneous goofing off.

So using our little formula, the amount you'd want to make would be $65,000 + (.30 x 65,000) = $84,500 gross pay for the year.

Admittedly you may be relieved to just be breaking even your first year or two. You certainly wouldn't be alone if break-even is the best you do your first twelve to twenty-four months; that's normal for a rookie. In fact, pulling in $65,000 your first year as a freelancer is pretty darned impressive. But once you get your freelance legs, you by all means should strive to make a profit. Subcontracting, raising your rates, and taking corporate work rank among the most popular ways to boost your earnings. We'll talk about all these later in the book. Meanwhile, let's finish figuring out your rate.

Time Off for Good Behavior

Besides not getting paid to prepare that estimate for HotShitStartup .com or file all the printouts scattered about our office floor, we freelancers don't get paid for the days we take off. So in order to come up with a true freelance rate, we need to plug into the equation the hours we'll actually be working this year.

I don't know about you, but I like at least a month off a year, preferably six weeks or more. How much vacation, sick, and holiday time you take is up to you, but most small business experts suggest a minimum of six or seven weeks. If you have small kids, for example, you may find you need two to four weeks alone for the days they're home from school with the flu.

So let's say you're planning to work 46 weeks a year. And since I'm a fan of having a life outside work, let's say you're going to work an average of 40 hours a week. As we've already established, you won't spend all those hours doing billable work. Most new freelancers find themselves trolling for work and keeping up with administrata up to half the week. But since I know you plan to hit the freelance trail with a few repeat clients in tow (right?), let's estimate that your first year freelancing full-time you'll bill clients for 60 percent (24 hours) of the 40-hour workweek. That means you'll bill for 1,104 hours a year (24 hours x 46 workweeks).

Now, to figure out what you need to make per hour, we divide that handy-dandy target income we arrived at earlier (not the break-even one, the one where you make a 30 percent profit) by the billable hours you'll work for the year. So $84,500 / 1,104 = $76.54 an hour, which we might as well round up to $80 an hour.

Not all freelancers bill by the hour. Massage therapists charge by session. Film producers charge by the day. Information architects often bill by project milestone. And writers often get paid by the word. In fact, as you'll see in Chapter 11, there are plenty of reasons *not* to bill by the hour. But figuring out the minimum amount per hour (or day, week, or month) that'll get you out of bed is essential. Once you know your bottom line, it's much easier to choose which clients to work for, estimate and negotiate project prices, and walk away when the deal stinks like six-day-old fish.

Again, depending on which freelancer you ask, $80 an hour is either a pauper's wage, highway robbery, or right on the money. A relatively new proofreader in the publishing industry might work for a quarter of that amount. A certified financial planner with ten years' experience might charge anywhere from $100 to $200 an hour. But to a novice graphic artist, $80 an hour might be just right.

There's only one way to find out if your rate will hold water in the freelance marketplace: see what your competitors are charging.

Keep Up with the Joneses

Whether you're a freelance translator, tax preparer, or taxidermist, there's a good chance someone's written a blog post or article on pricing tactics for the trade. And you know those other personal shoppers and pet psychics you scoped out on the web back in Chapter 1? Some of them will have their freelance rates posted right on their website. Others will mention the professional associations they belong to (Kansas City Knicker Knitters, Freelance Femmes of Fresno), many of which will offer lectures, workshops, and schmoozefests—all fine forums for uncovering what someone with your amount of experience in your industry (and located in your neck of the woods) stands to earn. Ditto for the free email discussion lists many of those professional associations offer. One caveat: Discussion list moderators won't let you talk prices in an online public forum (for fear of being accused of illegal "price fixing"), but you can always ask your fellow listmates to email you their scoop privately.

Be sure you get a sampling of opinions about what to charge for the type of work you do and the individuals or organizations you do it for. It would be a shame to rely on the advice of the one undercharger in the bunch. Some professional groups and web communities, like Mediabistro and FreelanceSwitch, publish surveys they've taken of their members' pricing practices—invaluable info to get your hands on.

In doing this research, you'll no doubt notice that Freelancer A doing the same type of work as you for a roster of Fortune 500 clients gets a considerably higher rate than Freelancer B, who mainly works for small-town nonprofit arts organizations. If you plan to work for a couple industries with vastly divergent budgets, you'll likely wind up with a couple different hourly rates: one for the crap-pay comedy night-club gigs you take, and one for the now-we're-talking corporate parties you emcee.

So how does your rate rate? If $80 an hour is twice as much as most freelancers with your level of experience are getting paid to do the same type of work you do, you may want to rethink your pricing. To lower the rate you calculated here, you may have to boost your hours, shrink your expenses, or add some higher-paying bread-and-butter work to your client mix.

And if all your freelance counterparts are getting paid $100 an hour, you might want to raise your price as well. Why leave people scratching their heads wondering what the catch to your bargain-basement price is? More important, why charge less than you have to?

I know it can be hard to put a price tag on your talents, services, and creations, but trust me, it gets easier with time. Sometimes I find it helpful to pretend I'm some badass, take-no-prisoners business manager whose sole purpose in life is to get me as much money as possible for my work. And while Michelle Goodman might be a bit timid when it comes to pricing, Mitzy Goodman is anything but a pushover.

Unlike supermodel Linda Evangelista, you may not be able to say it takes ten grand to rouse you out of bed in the morning. But knowing that you won't wake for less than $80, $100, or $150 an hour might just be the thing that saves you from a lifelong diet of celery and cigarettes.

PART 2

Sell, Baby, Sell

*Y*ou've outlined some goals for yourself, tricked out your home office, and gotten real with your finances. So what the heck do you do now, besides wait for your inbox to chime or cell phone to ring? How do you help yourself to a piece of the indie work pie, and just what the heck are you supposed to do and say once you get a nibble from a potential client?

So many freelancers—rookies and vets alike—will tell you that their criteria for finding clients is "whoever wants me, and whatever they're offering." But that's hardly good criteria. Yes, you need to eat. But cherry-picking your projects can make the difference between eating ramen and eating solid food. More important, it can make the difference between filling your plate with mercenary freelance work and making room for that "pinch me—I must be dreaming" creative work you've always wanted to do (most likely the reason you wanted to freelance in the first place).

Likewise, failing to negotiate project price and parameters (deadline, expenses, pay cycle) is a recipe for overwork and underpayment. I think you can see where I'm going with this: A passive freelancer does not a satisfied, well-fed creative professional make. So in this section, I'll show you how to be more strategic about the clients you get into bed with and the projects you accept, from first contact to signed contract.

Whether you're new to freelancing and need some clients in a jiffy or an old pro looking to punch up your existing client list, you'll get a meaty list of tips you can use to land new customers, build networking and marketing into your weekly routine, and channel your inner haggler. And if you're still trying to wriggle free from the 9-to-5 tie that binds, not to worry. Many of the suggestions packed into this section are things you can do online and on your own time.

Chapter 7

Fill Your Dance Card

Jump-start your client list: Bang on doors, build a freelance posse, and get in the referral game

"I told two friends about Fabergé Organics shampoo with pure wheat germ oil and honey, and they told two friends, and so on . . . and so on . . . and so on . . . "

—Shampoo commercial from the seventies

To give you an idea of how much indie work is out there, a 2007 CareerBuilder study found that 55 percent of companies had either hired or planned to hire freelancers or contractors in the near future. Sixty-four percent of them planned to hire solo workers during the second half of 2007. And 20 percent said they were hiring more indie professionals than they did a year ago thanks to a "shortage of qualified labor." We're not just talking about tech gigs; we're talking about finance, design, marketing, editorial, HR, admin, sales, and consulting work too.

So how do potential clients find players for their freelance dream team? Overwhelmingly, by referral—and not just from their 9-to-5 comrades. Often, clients look to their freelancers for referrals.

Let me share with you a little scene that plays out in my inbox on an almost weekly basis:

> *Hi, Michelle. It's your Favorite Deep-Pocketed Client here.*
> *Say, I know you're busy writing that book, but would you*
> *happen to have a freelance friend who does what you*

do and is available? I need to fill this slot in the next 48 hours. Let me know if you know anyone.

Or:

Hi, Michelle. It's your freelance BFF here. My editor at TwentyMillionCirculation *magazine needs someone to write an article on recovering Republicans who love too much and I don't have the time this month. Sounds like a fun story, and the pay is good. Let me know if you want an email introduction. I already gave her your contact info.*

Call it nepotism, favoritism, or the good old freelancer's club. I just call it smart. Harried clients who needed the work done yesterday don't have time to roll the dice by placing an ad on a site like Sologig.com and slogging through all those resumes. They know nobody knows more freelancers than we freelancers, so they ask us. Look what Kate Henne of Fargo, North Dakota, a freelance communications guru who spent fifteen years working as a marketing manager for major corporations, has to say on the matter:

"Most of the freelancers I've worked with have come by word of mouth. Sure, I want to see resumes/portfolios or just examples of work, but networking with reputable pros is invaluable. If you're a writer, get to know designers, web producers, project managers, et cetera, so you can recommend great resources when your client needs them. You'll develop a great network, and clients will know they can count on you to help keep projects running smoothly."

Forget the don't-fraternize-with-the-competition mentality. If a client like Kate calls me up and I'm short on time, skills, or interest in the job, there's no reason I wouldn't recommend a trusted indie pal who fits the gig description and is looking to fill a hole in her schedule. Hell, earlier this year a client sent me two thousand bucks, unsolicited, for suggesting two freelancers for long-term contracts he was desperate to fill. If that's not incentive to share and share alike, I don't know what is.

I've Got Friends in Freelance Places

How do you catapult yourself into this inner sanctum where all the referral magic happens? By befriending other solo workers. As soon as humanly possible. Don't wait till you're more experienced or outgoing or confident. You need the work now—not to mention the camaraderie of other indie workers—so start shaking hands *today*. Don't believe the myth that there's some Secret Referral Society that only admits free-lancing veterans. When a rookie I admire is trying to break in, I'm happy to recommend her to a client for a gig I can't do. So find out where the other freelancers in your neck of the woods congregate—online and in person—and don't walk there. Run.

Since online schmoozing doesn't require a tin of Altoids or much courage, start there: Search for local chapters of professional associa-tions that feature free email discussion lists—for example, Digital Eve, Professional Women of Color Network, and Graphic Artists Guild. Or subscribe to one of the countless lists on Yahoo! Groups. Hands down, these lists are among the best ways to find freelance gigs in your own back yard. To me, discussion lists are the virtual equivalent of at-tending a dinner party with several hundred of your most supportive freelance friends.

freelance tip

If you haven't already done so, cre-ate a signature for all your outgoing email messages. That way, when you post to these discussion lists people know who you are, where they can find your portfolio online, and how they can reach you. Keep it short and sweet; no one likes a nineteen-line sig or a "digital busi-ness card" attachment.

I'm on six email lists for West Coast writers and freelancers and see both freelance and long-term contract jobs listed every week—by other freelancers trying to help a client out, and by clients them-selves. Since many of these lists have just a couple hundred to a couple thousand members, there's less competition when you send in your resume. I've landed many a gig this way over the years, as have most freelancers I know.

Web communities, forums, and blogs for indie pros—Biznik, Mediabistro, Craftster, and FreelanceSwitch, to name a few—are also great places to meet freelance folks and pick up tricks of the trade. Some even feature job listings. I've listed a few favorites in the Resource Guide, too. And if you've got a spare hour or two, you might as well put your profile on Biznik, LinkedIn, or your online social network of choice. Joining a digital tribe makes approaching a freelance rock star with a question like "How did you make the leap from portrait photography to photojournalism?" about one hundred times easier.

Still, nothing helps friendships blossom like good old-fashioned face time, so you'll also want to start frequenting the popular brick-and-mortar freelance haunts near you—soon, like before the seasons change. And you'll want to conduct this hobnobbing at least once a month, especially while trying to fill your freelance schedule (and bank account). The easiest thing to do is check out some local happy hours, meetings, and talks hosted by your professional association or arts organization of choice—Women in Film, Weimaraner Walkers of Westchester, et cetera. Also see http://freelance.meetup.com to find (or create) a group of like-minded indies near you. Bring a friend as your wingwoman if you need support. If after one outing you're left thinking *These are definitely not my people,* try another event or organize a freelancers' happy hour of your own.

Don't overlook the value of rubbing elbows with professionals *outside* your field. There's something to be said for being the only caterer in a roomful of wedding planners. I know a software developer who gets a ton of referrals from the Graphic Artists Guild meetings she regularly attends, as well as a photographer who lands loads of work shooting same-sex weddings thanks to the LGBT business events she frequents.

As you venture out into the brave new freelance social circuit, don't just look for people you can leech information, contacts, and work off of, and don't expect handouts. Seasoned freelancers can smell a parasite a mile away. Bring your own sparkling wit, shimmering ideas, and innovative suggestions to the table, which, even if you're a newbie, you're bound to have. Take an interest in others, not just their Outlook address books. Repay favors any way you can. At the very least, buy an old salt a drink to show your appreciation for all the tips she's given you.

Where the Clients Are

Like Rome, your big fat freelance network won't be built in a day. Besides, it takes a lot more than charming the pants off other indie professionals to fill your freelance dance card. When it comes to jump-starting your client list, these are the tactics I've found work best:

TELL AUNT AGNES. If you haven't already done so, your first step should be to tell your aunt Agnes, cousin Carl, roommate Ruby, dog walker Derek, and anyone else you've ever spent thirty seconds sucking the same air with about your new freelance life. What one email reading "Hi, everyone. Did I mention I've struck out on my own as a freelance fortune-teller/futurist/food stylist?" can't cover, a brief face-to-face chat the next time you see the party in question, punctuated by the placement of your business card in her outstretched hand, can.

While friends can be a great source of freelance leads ("My boss was just saying yesterday we need to broaden our pool of freelance animators!"), friendships and invoices don't mix. So unless you feel comfortable asking your best bud of fifteen years the whereabouts of your check that's three weeks late, stick to working for her manager or officemates.

My first couple years working solo, my clients included a former college roommate's current roommate, a high school buddy's husband's start-up, a couple I met while photocopying something at Kinko's, and countless neighbors, friends of friends, and friends' bosses and coworkers. But it's not just me. Ask any freelancer how she got her first couple of clients and there's a good chance you'll hear a story like that of Elizabeth Mance, an Arthur Andersen expat who now runs Accountability Services, a Seattle-based accounting boutique for small business owners: "A neighbor who was a real estate agent was struggling with her tax return, and I said, 'I could do your tax return for you.' And before I know it, I had four clients from her brokerage firm who I was doing taxes for."

In fact, Elizabeth's decade-old business now gets more than 40 percent of its customers from the real estate industry—all because she told one neighbor. Ah, the power of the Fabergé Shampoo Commercial Principle.

RECYCLE OLD DANCE PARTNERS. Having your friends, family, and neighbors pimp you out is of course just part of the pavement-pounding story. Another tried-and-true for landing clients is to recycle as many former employers as you can. So if you didn't do so on your way out the door, tell any former managers and colleagues who didn't leave a foul taste in your mouth that you've struck out on your own and would be happy to lend a freelance hand. Email, call, fax, telegraph, send smoke signals, whatever it takes.

Remember to reach out to former coworkers and managers who have moved on to new companies. Ditto for organizations you've volunteered with or temped at, as well as any vendors you outsourced work to when you were back in the 9-to-5 grind. I've turned all of the above into clients over the years.

My first steady freelance gig was writing advertorials for a daily newspaper I'd interned for after college. I believe the initial phone conversation went like this: "Hi, Michelle. I hear you worked in our newsroom last summer writing mind-numbingly dull features about local legislation. I edit the newspaper's advertorial section, and I'm looking for a freelance writer to get the scoop on our biggest retail advertiser's fall clothing line and write some quick, pithy articles that basically tell people how to part with their hard-earned money at the mall. Oh, and we'll pay you as much for each piece as you make in a week at that pissant 9-to-5 admin job of yours with the gluey mousetraps under your desk that keep getting stuck to the bottom of your shoes...."

In other words, she had me at hello.

As we've already established, outsourcing managers live for referrals. If the freelance need exists, your contacts will be all over you like flies on stank. Not only are you a proven talent, you already know what all those obscure industry acronyms mean. Lest you think that returning to the nest is beneath you, I'd like to point out that early in 2008, former *Saturday Night Live* head writer Tina Fey guest-hosted *SNL* and reprised her role as Weekend Update co-anchor, proving that no matter how high on the creative ladder you climb, you're never too big to go home again.

COZY UP TO CREATIVE AGENCIES. Whether you write code, walk dogs, or wax floors, somewhere there's a contract agency with your name on it, from big firms like the international Aquent, Hired Guns in New York, and Filter on the West Coast, to smaller, more specialized outfits like WAM Marketing Group, the biomed ad agency mentioned in Chapter 5. If it weren't for the many editorial, technical documentation, and marketing agencies that over the years fed me everything from three-hour work-from-home projects to three-month full-time contracts on their clients' turf, I might have scurried back to the 9-to-5 grind long ago. The beauty of working with a creative agency—which functions much like a temp agency, only for freelancers and contractors—is they already have the clients and gigs in hand. The only missing ingredient is you.

Besides rounding out your schedule and income, taking agency work is a fine way to supersize your skills. Jocelyn Brandeis, who's been a freelance publicist in New York since 2001, gets about 30 percent of her work from bigger publicity agencies. Though her PR background is in corporate entertainment, she's worked with creative agencies to boost her experience in the nonprofit, retail, travel, tech, and wedding sectors. "When I send my resume or my bio to clients, they're really impressed that I have more general experience than just entertainment. The more experience I can get in other areas, the more clients I can work with," she says.

Another bonus of working as an agency subcontractor is you learn how to wheel and deal with clients by osmosis. That's what happened to Sheryl Landon, a freelance web application developer in Seattle who went solo after a post-9/11 layoff when, as she says, "I couldn't find a job to save my life." Because she works in what's probably the biggest "wait and hurry up" industry on the planet—"It's typical software development; projects either get behind or everyone shows up late," she says—there's a fair amount of client diplomacy involved around deadlines. Occasionally she had the chance to watch the principal of a small agency she'd been freelancing for finesse the client about delays in the project schedule ("Since you got us the source materials late, we'll need an extra week to finish the project"). For Sheryl, this was like a crash course in client negotiations.

Thanks to the agency work I've done in the past fifteen years—which, like Jocelyn, has totaled about 30 percent of my time—I've been able to add swanky titles like project manager, web community editor, and developmental book editor to my resume, as well as a few megacorp clients that would have been infinitely harder to infiltrate by my lonesome. Sure, agency work wasn't always my first choice, but it's helped me stay recession-proof all these years. And in some cases, it's led to future freelance work with clients I met through the agency (more on how to fairly finagle this in "When Noncompete Clauses Attack" in Chapter 12). Know that not all agencies are created equal. Some pay better and are more straight up than others. Some even offer health insurance, paid days off, and retirement fund matching. To find the best agencies near you, ask your fellow freelancers for recommendations.

CANVASS THE NEIGHBORHOOD. When Jocelyn began freelancing seven years ago, she embarked on some serious pavement pounding. "I just started knocking on doors in New York City," Jocelyn says. "If a new business opened up, I walked in there and said, 'Hi, I'm Jocelyn and I think you need PR for x, y, and z.'" Same goes for Laura Michalek, a former vintage furniture store owner who, in 2005, made the leap to full-time freelancing as a fundraising auctioneer. "You really have to create your own opportunities," she says. "Early on in my auction career, I not only had to convince folks to have an auctioneer, but an *auction.*"

But you needn't be a brazen publicist or lifelong saleswoman to do this. When I showed up in the San Francisco Bay Area without a client to my name, I cracked open the phone book (remember, this was 1992) and began randomly calling publishing companies to see if any needed freelance writing, editing, or proofreading help. Don't ask me how—I was as shy as a mouse back then. But I really, *really* did not want a day job. So I hyperventilated awhile and then picked up the receiver. I might have even done a shot of tequila. An hour later I had nineteen no's and one "send us your resume" from a company that soon became one of my most lucrative clients. Not bad for an hour's work, though if I'd been smarter I would have done what Ally Peltier, a freelance writer and editor in Baltimore, does:

"I often pick up fliers, newsletters, and postcards from workshop presenters, speakers, or other businesses advertising around town," she says. "More often than not, these materials are riddled with errors. I edit them and sometimes rewrite them, then send them to the originator with a note advertising my own services." Of course, you don't have to work as a wordsmith to try this trick. If you're a DJ, you can tactfully point out why no one was dancing to the tired old Kool & the Gang tracks at your local yoga studio's holiday fundraiser and send over an MP3 of your best Bollywood-inspired set. If you're a landscape designer, you can tell your neighborhood community center that their greenery's dying from sun, shade, or aphid overload and show them some choice photos of the lush courtyards you've designed.

No matter how you get your daily media dose (print, web, phone, TV, radio, microchip in your head), learn to love the local business news. It's the best way to see which regional organizations are making good, which corporate Goliaths are opening up a satellite office near you, and which midsize companies are expanding—all potential clients you can hit up for work.

Freelance Job Sites—the Good, the Bad, and the Ugly

While there are a lot of great job-hunting websites out there for freelancers, there's also a ton of garbage. Early in 2008, the directory AllFreelance.com listed several dozen freelance job sites, from catch-all sites like Sologig.com, Guru.com, FreelanceSwitch.com, and Elance.com to industry-specific sites like RentACoder.com and DesignQuote.com. Since freelance job sites come and go like a bad stomach flu, I'd rather not focus on which sites are good (or bad, or downright fugly), but on site practices, instead.

Let's look at the good first. I'm a big fan of narrowing the playing field from the globe to one geographic region (whether that region is your state, country, or continent). A majority of jobs listed on freelance sites can be done from anywhere—Indiana, India, Indonesia—which may sound like a good deal for you at first blush but couldn't be farther from it. Think about it: Would you rather be one of one hundred regional applicants or one of one thousand worldwide? Sadly, sites like Freelance-Seattle.net and FreelanceDirectory.org (for the UK and Ireland) are few and far between. So unless you see an ad for the solo gig of your dreams, I'd stick with region-specific ads on those national and worldwide sites.

Craigslist can be a speedy way to drum up local freelance leads. A number of freelancers I spoke to landed their first few freelance gigs through Craigslist. But you don't have to read a site like CraigslistCurmudgeon.com to know that countless freelance ads on Craig's venture into the territory of the seriously scary. Some easy ways to spot a Craig's dud: The ad doesn't say what the company name or website is or is incredibly vague. What's more, they promise to pay you not in cash dollar bills but in "exposure." (More about when to do free-bies in Chapter 10.) And my personal favorite, "To find out how you can make $8,000 a month working from home, call this 800 number for a recorded message. Please have your credit card ready ..." Trust your gut. If it sounds like a scam, don't bother.

Then there are the subscription-based job sites, of which I've seen both good and bad. Since nonfiction writers land a lot of their assignments by pitching ideas to magazine, web, and newspaper editors, nominally priced subscriptions to sites like Mediabistro and FreelanceSuccess—both of which offer current leads and professional advice—can pay for themselves quickly. But some other sites cost hundreds of dollars to join annually. For your money, you may get some services that ensure your clients pay up, but this involves giving the site your tax ID (social security) number and routing your invoices and payments through them, which gives me the willies. Even if you have no other work, there are better ways to spend your money. For more marketing ideas, see Chapter 18.

As for the out and out ugly, a lot of these freelance sites are set up like one big job auction. A potential client lists a gig and then eBay-style bidding ensues, only in reverse, with each freelancer offering to do it cheaper than the next. Not only that, you may have to bid on projects you know diddly about, which can further reduce your rate if the client's project description doesn't match the reality. Equally hideous are the design contest sites where freelancers create logos and web pages on spec (for free) and the "client" picks a winner to receive a piddly cash award. If you want to do charity work, you're better off picking an organization you know and love.

I can't stress this enough: A personal connection or recommendation trumps applying for a gig cold every time. So before you start scouring the jobs boards and blindly applying for gigs, make sure you've looked in every nook and cranny of your personal and professional network.

I know this chapter covered a lot of ground, so don't feel like you have to try every last client-hunting tactic mentioned here. When it comes to trolling for gigs, anything goes. One freelancer might be a referral whore who loves to hobnob at industry parties (guilty as charged), while the next might thrive on scouring the business pages, job boards, and discussion lists and swooping in on some of the more promising-sounding opportunities she sees.

"Seventy-five percent of my new clients come from referrals, either from existing clients or editing colleagues," says Sherri Schultz, a freelance editor in San Francisco who's worked solo for sixteen years. "So all the initial stress of sending out resumes and calling to follow up— or not calling to follow up because it was so nerve-racking—or stressing because I felt I *should* send out resumes but was putting it off—it's pretty much a complete waste of time."

As Sherri points out, *shoulding* yourself is highly overrated. If you keep striking out with Craigslist, are loath to use LinkedIn, or would rather eat a pile of paper clips than contact a creative agency, by all means skip it—especially if your dance card's filling up fast with projects that make you swoon. Just promise me you won't skimp on building a community of freelance comrades. Believe me, after six weeks of working solo in your skivvies, you'll be grateful for the company, digital or otherwise.

Chapter 8

Choose Clients Wisely, Grasshopper

Don't just tread water—cherry-pick your projects

"Contrary to popular opinion, the hustle is not a new dance step—it's an old business procedure."

—Fran Lebowitz, *The Observer*, 1979

I'll forever remember Mrs. Crowell, my grade school music teacher with the bleached blond hair and psychedelic neckerchiefs, for two things.

One: She pissed off my feminist mom by making all the girls in my class perform Rodgers and Hammerstein's "I Enjoy Being a Girl," complete with jazz hands, at one of those evening chorus recitals music teachers like to make children and their parents suffer through.

Two: The movie *Superman* had just come out, and everyone was creaming their jeans over Christopher Reeve. Apparently Mrs. Crowell had a tall, dark, and dashing brother with a cowlick who was a struggling model/actor and a dead ringer for Reeve. And apparently her brother had been second or third or perhaps two-hundredth in line for the part of ole blue tights, a fact Mrs. Crowell never missed an opportunity to share with the class. Thing is, we didn't care.

Even as a kid, it struck me as sad that Mrs. Crowell couldn't let go of the gig that got away (from her brother, no less). From the way she went on and on about it, I wondered if her brother had been boozing it up in some dingy hotel room for the past six months, his cowlick unsprung from lack of showering, a Chris Reeve dartboard on the wall, and the Brando line "I could have been a contender" looping in his head.

What Mrs. Crowell failed to realize is that you can't hitch your entire creative career on one big break—or one fat failure. When you don't get a callback, you can't dwell on the defeat too long. And if you do land the starring role, you can't let yourself get too comfortable or complacent. You have to keep moving forward, reaching for bigger and better. After all, you've got a business to run. Bills to pay. Bacon to bring home. Dreams to put in motion. Big, juicy "look out, world, here I come" dreams.

The Hunt for Repeat Customers

Remember that Business Plan To Go you wrote back in Chapter 1? And how you figured out how much money you need to earn per year back in Chapter 6? These are the details you need to keep in mind as you head off to harvest new clients. The more strategic you are about choosing who to work with and which projects you take, the better your business will do—and the sooner you'll meet those creative, professional, and financial goals you made in Part 1 of the book.

"It used to seem so crass to me to do your creative work with your financial compensation in mind or having that be such a major component of the process," says graphic artist Ellen Forney. "But it is, because it's your living now. And it affects how much time you can put into it. And ideally what it's doing is giving you enough time so that you can do whatever work it is that you find most satisfying, which by and large doesn't pay well. You have to take good-paying gigs in order to do the work you find most satisfying."

Like Ellen, it took me a while to wrap my mind around the whole craft plus commerce concept. Back in the nineties, I had this friend with a 9-to-5 gig selling magazine ads in Silicon Valley. More than once she ended a phone call to me with "Let me talk to you later—I gotta go find another $50,000 by Friday ..." At the time, I thought, *Ugh, ad sales—could there be anything more heinous?* But supporting yourself as a freelancer means thinking like my friend the sales hound. You have to weigh the target income you came up with in Chapter 6 against how much work you have on deck each month. If you're a week into the month and you have a $2,500 hole in your schedule, it's time to get cracking.

I realize that when you're in pavement-pounding start-up mode and someone offers you a hundred bucks to massage their copy, boost their website's Google rank, teach their old dog new tricks, or whatever it is you do best, your first inclination will probably be to say "How soon can I start?" Depending how low your checking account balance is, you may have no choice but to say yes and help yourself to a slice of that buttered bread.

But keep in mind that each new client you get into bed with requires an investment of your time. You need to learn your way around their likes, dislikes, mission, lingo, and all those industry-specific trends. And each project you take on comes with its very own set of unpaid administrative tasks, from contract negotiations to invoicing to record keeping. I don't know about you, but I'd rather manage four $1,000 jobs a month than forty $100 jobs—a handful of clients is much easier to juggle than several dozen.

One way you can eliminate piecemeal work and the accompanying administrative avalanche is to set a minimum project price (or session time, if you're, say, a therapist or business coach). During my first couple freelance years, I wouldn't take a gig for less than $250, even if the project was to write a three-paragraph press release. (My minimum is about four times that now.) It simply wasn't worth the ramp-up and admin time. As Seattle web designer Colleen Lynn says, "If you want me to really build an effective site, I'm going to have to understand your audience. I'm going to have to understand the market. And that means research." Her bottom line? "If my first project for a new client isn't worth $3,000, I'm going to eat it."

In the interest of staying solvent, you'll also want to find as many repeat clients as possible. For this reason, I prefer to work with multi-employee companies over individuals. A life coach might ask me to revise her web copy once a year. But my midsize business and megacorp clients have journalism or copywriting needs throughout the year. "We're looking to increase our freelance pool" is something you'll hear a lot as you begin to do the mating dance with more and more clients. And if you don't, there's nothing wrong with asking what freelance needs the client has coming down the pipeline, how often they out-source work, or what their freelance budget is. (For more help turning first-time clients into repeat customers, see Chapter 13.)

On the flip side, you don't want to become too dependent on one client (or for that matter, the agency work we talked about in Chapter 7). Don't be the freelancer who sucks on the teat of one cash cow, leav-ing no time for other work (and no time to scratch your creative itch). In the mid-nineties, that was me. I'd spent two years writing marketing copy and editing books almost exclusively for a small California-based technical book publisher. Without warning, the firm was sold and swal-lowed up by a giant publisher in the Midwest, leaving me and the com-pany's other freelancers twisting in the wind. Suddenly I had a sinkhole where my jam-packed schedule used to be and had to scramble to put some new gigs together.

In retrospect, losing that cash cow was the greatest thing that ever happened to me as a freelancer. I'd become complacent, bored, and burned out, and I'd stopped making time for the fun writing gigs I en-joyed most. But three weeks after my cash cow bought the farm, I had a shiny new client list, complete with a couple of more creative, less vanil-la projects. I was a freelancer reborn. Suddenly work was fun again. So let this be a lesson to you: No client should account for more than a third of your revenue each year. And not just for financial reasons, but to keep your creative, variety-loving self energized about your work. Because isn't that why you want to be your own boss in the first place?

Specialize or Starve!

Early on in my freelance career, I did a lot of dabbling until I found a couple commercial writing niches that held my interest and fueled my bank account best. My first couple boss-free years, I did much more PR writing—and even a handful of start-to-finish publicity campaigns, complete with pitching story ideas to the press on behalf of my artist/author/musician clients—before realizing I couldn't stand doing PR. I also tried my hand at writing infomercials and scripts for authors looking to adapt their work to audio, neither of which appealed to me and both of which I sucked at.

When a few years into my business I finally sank my teeth into copywriting and editing for book publishers, dot-coms, and software companies, I knew I'd found my home, at least on the bread-and-butter side of things. On the creative side, finding my home was much easier. From the get-go, I wrote articles and essays about things I knew and loved: alt careers, self-employment, dating, mating, and dogs.

But honing your expertise and cultivating a couple of specialties doesn't just help you stay at the top of your game, it helps you stay gainfully employed. Clients don't have the time to teach a freelancer about the nuances of their industry, product, or subject matter. They want to hire someone who's been there and designed, edited, photographed, built, trained, tested, or healed that, someone who can hit the proverbial ground running. Build up a niche or three for yourself, and suddenly you're a hot commodity. In a crowded creative marketplace, you'd be wise to set yourself apart from the pack this way.

"Typically when I pick up clients in niches, I start picking up all their friends," says Denver-based personal trainer Alisa Geller, who works with a lot of ballet dancers, people training for triathlons, and people with MS. Likewise, because I have more than a decade of experience writing and editing for the software industry, I get far more freelance gigs and can command a higher rate for editorial tech work than a writer/editor who doesn't know a router from a Roto-Rooter. But Alisa and I don't hold a monopoly on niche building. Laura Michalek, the auctioneer you met in Chapter 7, specializes in fundraising events for nonprofits, community groups, and schools. Interior designer Piper Lauri Salogga specializes in feng shui, green design, and home offices. You get the idea.

Having a specialty doesn't mean you have to pigeonhole yourself. In fact, to stay in the black, cultivating an assortment of skills, services, or products within your niche is a must. "Most illustrators that I know also do web design or animation or teach or some combination," says illustrator Nina Frenkel, who does everything from illustrating children's books to animating music videos to teaching at the college level. "And I don't find that a bummer or a sell-out or a sad thing. I find that very exciting that all of these different things feed each other."

Empty Niche Syndrome

Not sure what to specialize in? Start by asking yourself these questions:

- What topics, products, causes, services, and industries excite me most?
- Which ones pay the best?
- Which have I always wanted to learn about?
- What contacts and skills do I already have in place that I can capitalize on?
- How can I improve on what other freelancers in my line of work are doing?
- How can I offer something different (a new service, a unique product, a creative approach to my craft) so I stand out from the crowd?

That's not to say a niche you begin building today has to be one you see yourself in a decade from now. So if you still have a day job and can do your early spelunking on your employer's dime, you absolutely should. Volunteer for as many types of projects as you can to see what you love, hate, tolerate, rock at, suck at. For example, if you're an interior designer, design everything from doctors' waiting rooms to nonprofit conference rooms to CEOs' living rooms. If you're a technically inclined editor, edit scientific journals, software help files, case studies for the telecom industry, and anything else you can get your hands on. Collect client testimonials and start filling up your portfolio. Don't wait till you're working solo like I did if you don't have to. If, however, you're already in the freelance game and looking to build a new niche from the ground up, it's time to start dabbling, my friend.

One caveat: There is such a thing as having too many "specialties." During my brief stint as a freelance publicist, one of my musician clients had

⇨

⇨

a business manager who was also a practicing lawyer, financial consultant, concert promoter, motivational speaker, and copywriter, with a couple different product lines he was trying to get off the ground. The guy had about six different business cards, and it took him ten minutes to sum up what he did for a living. As he told it, he was hedging his bets to see which arm of his "business" took off first.

To me, that's not nursing a handful of specialties; that's playing the roulette wheel. It also comes off as incredibly fishy, not to mention anything *but* professional. Spread yourself too thin and you lose the ability to call yourself an expert in anything. To reap the marketing and financial rewards of specializing, you have to have the time to cultivate those niches. There's nothing wrong with pursuing more than one trade, industry, or subject matter. I've met plenty of people with titles like lawyer/grant writer, caterer/event planner, personal shopper/real estate stager, DJ/voice-over artist, dog walker/house sitter/plant doctor, blogger/dominatrix.

My rule of thumb: If you can't fit it all on one business card or sum it up in thirty seconds, you're probably a generalist.

It all comes back to that bread-and-butter safety net I've been talking about. "Though I feel spread thin at times, I try to keep a diversity of beats—even if I'm just doing the occasional off-topic article, in the event I need it later—to keep myself recession-proof," says Seattle-based business reporter Jane Hodges. "I consider doing this a very minor gesture compared to getting stuck and having to go back to some full-time job I don't want. So I write mostly about business and real estate, but I also write on mergers and acquisitions, astrology, and personal finance. If one of those industries shrinks editorial demand for coverage, I can shift emphasis and spend more time writing about the other topics without a lot of upheaval."

Diversifying also means keeping on top of the latest tech innovations in your field. Forget publish or perish—today it's blog/vlog/podcast/download or perish. Considering how rapidly the delivery media of film, music, software, journalism, visual arts, broadcasts, and anything else you can create is changing, we freelancers would be fools not to keep one foot in the digital pool. If you're not up on the latest business trends, start skimming the business pages. Or use Google alerts to get pinged with news stories on your industries of choice. If you're only targeting dying business models like pay phone companies for clients, it won't be long till you're SOL and out of work. Look to the future, my fellow Luddite, and make sure you have a healthy amount of sustainable customers on your dance card.

Channel Your Inner Nancy Reagan (Just Say No!)

Part of strategically shopping for clients and cultivating a specialty (or three) is learning to turn down the gigs that don't fit in with your master plan. This should come naturally when someone offers you minimum-wage pay or asks you to work on an ad campaign for, say, keeping teenage girls barefoot and pregnant (believe it or not, it's happened to me). Usually, though, the distinction between "right up my alley" and "not really my thing" isn't so clear-cut. The pay might be good, the client might be reputable, but the job is longer, shorter, bigger, smaller, more technical, less technical, duller, or more vanilla than what you normally do. Or it's a one-off gig for a one-time client in an obscure industry that doesn't warm your heart and won't pad your portfolio in any way. Or you used to do that kind of work but are trying to move away from it now.

Wedding photographer Anne Ruthmann, who lives in a small Indiana town but shoots all over the country, gets a lot of calls from couples who want traditional, posed, supermodel-for-a-day shots. Since she's more a candid, action-shot kind of gal, she refers those clients to a photographer who does what they're looking for. "I am not their photographer. I may show them at their most embarrassing moment. But I'm going to paint a very realistic and loving picture of them," she says.

Turning down some of the gigs you're offered might be scary at first. And if you haven't worked in three weeks and haven't eaten in three days, I wouldn't advise it. But if you're not starved for work or sustenance, remember that twenty hours spent on a "not really my thing" project is twenty hours you could have spent looking for a gig that's more in line with your master plan.

"Saying no has become one of my greatest strengths because I've been able to work by and large with people I love to work with," says Anne, who's been working solo for three years. "And they're hiring me for me, not just because I'm a photographer and I'm available."

In other words, channeling Nancy Reagan can make the difference between dreading and loving Mondays.

Do Try This at Home: Top Ten Client List

Resist the urge to put off handpicking your clients until you're more established, better paid, or better known. And don't listen to anyone who says you can't carve out a new niche if you didn't immerse yourself in the wonderful world of travel journalism, pet care, or consumer electronics straight out of school. Like an aging pop star, you can always reinvent yourself. At any point in your career. No high-price publicist needed.

And forget about silly twentieth-century marketing hangovers like blanket-mailing ten thousand brochures to every business within a sixty-mile radius. Your time's better spent making a short list of clients you want to work for and doing your darnedest to win them over. Even if you've been freelancing awhile, I encourage you to do this little exercise. It's all too easy to get stuck in the steady-money, bread-and-butter rut and forget why you came here. (Does "variety of projects, bigger and better clients, and time for your own creative work" ring a bell?)

So get out your pencils, people, because it's time to make a Top Ten list of the companies or individuals you'd most like to land as clients in the next year or two. Be sure to split your list evenly between fantasy clients you'd work for no matter what the pay (living-the-dream work) and hotshit commercial clients that will make your resume shine and bank account swell (bread-and-butter work). For example:

BREAD-AND-BUTTER LIST

1 Sassy & Sassy Advertising

2 Woohoo.com

3 Jill Bakes Foundation

And so on . . .

LIVING-THE-DREAM LIST

1 *Working Mama* magazine

2 *McSweetpea's* lit journal

3 Scallions.com satire news site

And so on . . .

Aim high, but don't aim so high that you need an industrial crane to reach the clients on your wish list. It's great that you want to see your cartoons grace the pages of *The New Yorker* or your photos published in *National Geographic*. But if to date you've only sold your work to your cul-de-sac's eight-page newspaper, you might want to aim for a few customers within reach first, like your city's daily metro paper, alt weekly, monthly magazine, or Gothamist-style news blog.

Once you've come up with your wish list, take some time each week—one hour, two hours, whatever you can spare—to chip away at it. Read about your dream clients online and see what the media's saying about them. See if anyone you've ever met in your life might have a contact at any of these organizations. See if any of your dream clients are advertising for the staff version of what you do as a freelancer, which you should definitely capitalize on. Then figure out the best way to approach them (see Chapter 9 for tips).

Whether you're just starting out or rolling in referral work, build this time into your weekly or monthly schedule, just as you would a dinner date or massage appointment. Write it in your calendar, set an alarm on your computer, whatever you need to do so you don't blow it off. If you land a client on the list, cross it off and add another. Don't wait until you have no work to boost your client base.

Even though I'm more than happy with the work on my plate, I've got goals, baby. So I make the time—be it Friday night or Sunday morning—to research and contact new clients I'd sell my right kidney to work with. I'll often spend an hour or two each week pursuing my dream clients, and much more if I find my workload dwindling or myself growing stagnant.

Even now, as I'm racing toward the finish line with writing this book, I'm collecting potential new client names, stockpiling article ideas, and lining up work for when I'm done. The way I see it, if you're not continually marketing yourself and climbing the client food chain, you're just treading water.

Chapter 9

Sales Pitch 101
How to seal the deal, from first contact to signed contract

"Put that coffee down! Coffee's for closers only."

—Alec Baldwin in *Glengarry Glen Ross*, 1992

I 've never read a book on selling or taken one of those Bag More Customers Now™ seminars. In fact, just thinking about the word "sales" makes me want to take a bath with a cheese grater. But unless you can afford a pimp, the cold reality of freelancing is you have to convince people to hire you, over and over and over again. You either learn to embrace your inner Alec Baldwin (albeit a kinder, gentler version), or you don't get to buy groceries.

Like many wide-eyed creative types, when I first struck out on my own at age twenty-four, I was blissfully ignorant of how much self-whoring I'd have to do. Pretty laughable when you consider that back then I was a wallflower—on a good day. You know the dinner party guest most likely to hide in the laundry room because she has no idea how to strike up a conversation, even with a friend of a friend she's met forty-five times? The ridiculously shy girl pretending to busy herself at the buffet table, terrified to look anyone in the eye, let alone speak in a register above a stage whisper? That was me.

Fortunately, trying to get people to hire you for a freelance gig isn't too different from trying to get someone to hire you for a staff job, something my mama mercifully taught me to do. "Nice to meet you, here's my bio, this is how I can help your company, and here's why I'm the right person for the job" still applies. So if you know how to ace a job interview, you know how to appeal for a freelance gig. (If you don't know how to interview, there are entire bookstore shelves devoted to that subject.)

That's not to say I was the Queen of Smooth. Queen of Awkward was more like it. As if the not-looking-people-in-the-eye thing wasn't disconcerting enough, my potential clients were often treated to bouts of nervous giggling, hair twirling, and cuticle picking. Ditto for my tendency to choke on my free coffee upon being asked "What's your availability?" or "So how much do you charge?" (Lesson number one: Don't negotiate over hot liquids.)

Whether my first few paying clients felt sorry for me, were worried about a scalding-induced lawsuit, or desperately needed a warm body, no matter how bumbling, is anybody's guess. Somehow, I managed to get enough of them to hire me that I kept my geeky ass out of the cube farm. And with each passing year, and each addition to my portfolio, I grew more poised, confident, and comfortable in my own freelance skin. Today I no longer hyperventilate before that initial phone call or meeting with a hotshot new client. And I must admit, sometimes I even get a little adrenaline rush out of hawking myself or my projects.

How to Make First Contact

But maybe you don't have the luxury of time. You're newer to this freelance game and you want to know what you can do *now* to polish your pitch, artfully woo potential new clients, and seal the deal. (If you're a shy introvert, you may even be wondering how you can become a sassy self-promoter overnight.) Thanks to a little game I like to play called Learn from My Cringeworthy Mistakes, you don't need to spend a decade-plus learning as you go like I did.

Let's start with contacting a client cold from that Top Ten list you made in Chapter 8. As anyone who's ever wasted her time blindly emailing jobs@wesellwidgets.com will attest, you need the name of the go-to person. Here's where that vast personal and professional network we talked about in Chapter 7 comes in handy. With any luck, you'll discover that your neighbor's boyfriend's cousin works at Sassy & Sassy Advertising and is happy to give you the name of an art director there who hires freelancers. Bonus points if your neighbor's boyfriend's cousin will talk you up to that art director or make an email introduction. And if tapping your network gets you nowhere, try your dream client's website, Google, LinkedIn, or everyone's favorite twentieth-century trick: calling up the company and asking for the name of the manager to contact about freelance work.

Trying to infiltrate a 25,000-employee megacorp without a personal recommendation or introduction can be a lot like trying to find a contact lens in a swimming pool. There is no contact info on the company website, no person you can call to ask about freelance opportunities. Often these companies outsource their work not to individual freelancers, but to those creative agencies we talked about in Chapter 7, who then hire the needed freelancers. So your job is to find out what staffing agencies the corporate empire you covet uses and to infiltrate *them*. Considering that half your town has probably worked for said empire at some point in their lives, you won't have to play Sherlock too long before you stumble on the right agencies to contact.

Once you get a contact name, use it as soon as humanly possible, while the introduction your friend made is still fresh and before your newfound contact ups and leaves for another job. Don't call; email. It's much less painful and much more efficient. "Back when I started up, there wasn't even any email," says author and *Los Angeles Times* columnist Meghan Daum. "So you used to have to pick up the phone and call an editor and pitch them, and they would answer and there was a horrible moment when they didn't know who you were and it was so humiliating."

Not only is email easier on you, it's about one hundred times less intrusive for the potential client. I don't know about you, but I don't take kindly to people interrupting my workday with unsolicited phone or—*horrors!*—doorstep sales pitches. Besides, an email gives you a nice, neat space to lay out your credentials, portfolio, and contact info for people to peruse at their convenience. Trust me, the last thing you want to hear when you've just got up the nerve to contact Sassy & Sassy is "What was your name again? Can you spell that? Wait, hang on a sec . . . Sorry, my pen just ran out . . . "

So what do you say? Quickly identify yourself, say how you got their name, and butter 'em up in a non-stalkerly way ("Loved your 'Real Women Have Curves' ad campaign," or "Kudos on nabbing a Clio—much deserved!"). Then tell them that you'd like to work with them and how you differ from all the other freelance photographers or copywriters out there (ten years on staff at ad agencies, experience working on big oil *and* green energy ad campaigns, et cetera). Don't get too carried away trying to sell them on how great you are; focus on what you can do to make *their* life easier. The whole email should be two to three short paragraphs max. And forget attachments. Instead, point them toward your website, where they can see your bio, samples, and client testimonials.

The Fine Art of Following Up

Don't be surprised if you don't hear back. Between spam filters and overflowing inboxes, there's a decent chance you won't. That's why you're going to follow up. Seriously. It helps grease the wheels, and it shows the client you mean business. I like to wait a week (not too soon, but not too long) and then forward the original email with an added, "Hello Client of My Dreams, just want to make sure you received the below email about my interest in freelancing for you. If I don't hear back from you by Friday, I'll give you a call next week."

Calling instead of emailing that first follow-up works, too. When dialing for dollars, keep it short and sweet. Quickly introduce yourself and then ask if they have a few minutes to chat before forging ahead with "Did you get my email?" Consideration for your contact's time goes a long way.

Follow their lead: If they sound frazzled, make it snappy. Potential clients don't have time to chitchat about *American Idol* or meet you for lunch so you can gas on about all the awards you've won or clients who've licked your boots. If they tell you to call back tomorrow, say "You got it!" and add it to tomorrow's to-do list. If they invite you downtown to show off your portfolio, oblige. If they tell you to try back again in three months, mark your calendar so you remember to follow through. If they tell you to go away, skedaddle. And if you don't reach them on your second attempt, wait another week or two before you give it one last go—by phone.

Timing is everything. The tax prep sector is slammed mid-February through mid-April. The book publishing world goes dormant in August and December. Retailers, craftsters, and indie manufacturers are crazy-busy with the holiday rush from Halloween on. Likewise, clients may be more apt to make freelance assignments earlier in the fiscal year (that is, once they've had their annual freelance budget okayed by the higher-ups). Catch a company on a tight budget during the last fiscal quarter and you might hear that they've already shot their financial wad for the year. So learn your way around the business cycles of the industries you're contacting and choose your moments wisely.

When it comes to follow-ups, I have a three-strike policy. If I've left three unanswered messages for one contact, I take that as my cue to cut bait. Pesky Freelancer is the last thing I want on my tombstone. Maybe I'll have some better, more relevant portfolio pieces six to nine months down the line and will send the contact in question the relevant links then, along with an email congratulating them on their latest industry achievement. Maybe I'll unearth a new contact at the company later in the year and try again. Maybe my original contact will crawl out of her cave eight months after receiving my initial missives and assign me a project (it's happened). Or maybe I'll just move on to bigger and better and not fret about it.

Let's say you get a nibble. And let's say that before you've even talked project parameters the client asks the fateful question, "What's your rate?" Unless your fee is an unflagging $125 an hour or $200 an afternoon because you sell your time in sessions (say, as a speech pathologist, fashion photographer, or SAT tutor), don't commit to a rate then and there. Suggesting an hourly rate or flat project fee without knowing the nature, complexity, and scope of the work is financial suicide. You can, however, offer up a price range:

"Depending on the complexity of the documents you want me to edit (consumer-facing web copy vs. scientific case study) and the level of editing required (light copyedit for grammar and consistency vs. heavier line-by-line revisions) my rate ranges from $65 to $90 an hour." Or, "The website applications I've built over the past two years have ranged in price from $5,000 to $25,000 depending on project scope. I'll be better able to give you an estimate once we go over specifics of the work you need done."

Got it? In other words, "I promise to not commit highway robbery, Dear Client of My Dreams, but you've got to give me a little information about the work you need done before I give you some firm numbers." Which is a perfect lead-in to a gentle "Do you have a specific project in mind you need help with? I'd be happy to go over the details with you and give you an estimate." (We'll dig deeper into estimating and negotiating project price in Chapter 11.)

How to Prod a Foot Dragger

Cousin to the client who wants to know how much it'll cost before there's even a project on the table is the client who says she wants you for an upcoming gig but drags her feet on giving you a start date or actually kicking off the project. Maybe you've already agreed to the project price and parameters by phone or email, but you left the start date loosey-goosey because the client didn't quite have all her ducks in a row. And now you're stuck waiting for your hopeful client to read the contract you sent her or send you the files she's supposedly hiring you to test, index, or Photoshop. And waiting. And waiting. And starting to wonder if this gig is ever going to get off the ground or if you should line up some other work instead.

As this is an all-too-common freelance occurrence, I don't consider any project with a new client—or an existing client who doesn't have all the project particulars worked out—a done deal until I have the work or contract in hand. (More on contracts in Chapter 12.) Projects get bogged down by red tape all the time. Maybe the client's waiting for some bean counter to cough up the project budget, or for a client of her own to deliver the files she needs to get to you. Or maybe a more pressing project was dumped in your client's lap and she's a bit deluged at the moment.

So what can you do to prod a foot dragger like this? A friendly nudge peppered with some "I'm here to help you, Oh Client of My Dreams!" charm usually does the trick. I like to call or send an email that says, "I know you said you need me to write that web copy sometime next month and that you just needed to get the paperwork [contract, money] together before we start. I'm starting to book up quick for [the next month, and the one after that] and want to make sure I leave room in my schedule for you. Ready to dance?"

Most of the time this lights a fire under the client's butt and the project is handed off to me within a week. But if "next month" is two weeks away and my contact still doesn't have it together, I won't hold her place in line—I'll give it to another client who has the money and assignment in hand.

Though this client mating game may sound nerve-racking, you've got to play it cool, lest you scare off your shiny new lead. It sounds so basic, but you'd be surprised how many new freelancers forget to breathe. Herewith three things you should never do, unless you're hell-bent on losing the gig:

FOLLOW UP EVERY HOUR ON THE HOUR. If the answer was "I don't have an answer for you yet" this morning, that's probably still the answer this afternoon. Patience, my freelance friend.

GO OVER YOUR CONTACT'S HEAD. Unless you have reason to suspect your would-be client quit, was canned, or has been hospitalized, don't ring up her boss to see why she hasn't sealed the deal with you yet. Not only will this piss off your contact *and* her boss, it will make you sound desperate.

SEND A CONTRACT BEFORE YOU HAVE AN ACTUAL YES. Ditto for starting the work before the client's given you the green light. Jumping the gun will warm your client's heart about as much as a dip in the Bering Sea.

What Doesn't Make You Race Back to the Cube Makes You Stronger

Obviously your leads won't always pan out. Some contacts will shoot you down or ignore you altogether. Others will say they want to work with you but bail before sealing the deal due to bureaucratic snags (freelance budget cutbacks), personnel changes (leading to budget cutbacks), or changes in their to-do list (courtesy of budget cutbacks). Turning even 10 percent of your leads into freelance gigs is truly something to celebrate. And a 50 to 75 percent success rate is party-like-it's-1999 fabulous.

Your mission, should you choose to accept it, is to try your darnedest to avoid taking the rejections personally. This isn't dating. It's business. Even freelancers who've had their share of successes have to deal with rejection at times. Los Angeles–based writer and improv goddess Lauren Weedman, who's performed half a dozen of her one-woman shows onstage throughout the country and has been a regular on such Comedy Central classics as *The Daily Show* and *Reno 911!,* told me this story about her trouble finding an agent:

"People wanted me for writing but not on camera, which is basically like being told to your face you're ugly. I went to Aspen in this comedy festival, which is a really hard festival to get into. This was like five years ago. I was on the fucking *Daily Show* at the time. And agents were telling me, 'Well, we only take writer/performers when they're people like Tina Fey.' Like, you've got to be an absolute proven double whammy. And, 'We want you for writing,' because they don't think your look is that marketable. That was so dizzying to have to hear over and over and again." (Happily, Lauren's since landed a great agent, not to mention some kick-ass new film and TV gigs.)

Moral of the story: The thickest of skins is required. If you find yourself daunted or discouraged by the no's, Google "famous rejections." Then take solace in all the famed writers, artists, musicians, inventors, and entrepreneurs who endured many a slamming door in the face before they became a household name. The sooner you too learn to eat your rejections for lunch (and believe me, there will be a whole buffet table to choose from), the better off you'll be.

In the meantime, how do you dull the sting of rejection? My favorite way is not to wallpaper my office with them or fashion them into an A-line dress or pay Lulu.com $90 to turn them into a roll of toilet paper. It's to keep putting myself out there, keep contacting the dream clients on my wish list, keep wheeling and dealing and dancing and charming and juggling as fast I can. The more balls I have in the air, the less I seem to mind the ones I miss.

Chapter 10

The Check Is *Not* in the Mail
When to give it up for free— and when to run for the nearest exit

"I'm an experienced woman. I've been around ... Well, alright, I might not've been around, but I've been ... nearby."

—Mary Tyler Moore in *The Mary Tyler Moore Show*, 1970

"You need experience to get experience." If you've been freelancing at least five minutes, you're no doubt familiar with this maddening old saw. Truth is, when trying to break into a new niche or business sector without the relevant work samples, sometimes you have to drop your drawers and bend over a little—metaphorically speaking, of course. And unless you're prepared to go back to a day job to get the necessary samples, the quickest way to flesh out a lean portfolio is to do a couple of freebie or low-paying gigs.

"Recently, I've been trying to break into technical writing and catalogs," says Ally Peltier, the Baltimore-based freelance writer/editor you met in Chapter 7, who went solo after working on staff for five years as a book editor. "A local freelancer had begun a project she didn't have time to finish and asked me if I was interested, giving me the opportunity to work with an IT company who was putting together a catalog. The rate was significantly lower than I would normally charge, but I took the job anyway, knowing that this was just a foot in the door. Next time, I'll have a great piece from my portfolio to show, and I'll be able to charge more."

Avoid doing freebie or heavily discounted work for any commercial clients on your wish list or any deep-pocketed industry rock stars you hope to forge a long-term, financially lucrative relationship with as a freelancer. Negotiating up from nothing or from a fraction of what you should be getting paid is a long road. Besides, if you give away your services or grossly underprice them, your dream clients may see you as not ready for prime time. Better to get your dress-rehearsal work from smaller organizations that could use a financial break and may not have the budget to pay your full rate: a pet shelter, a public radio station, or the new fair trade café/gallery down the street.

When donating your time or cutting someone a deal, be sure to let them know they're getting your "friends and family" rate, without lording it over them. "I've done some lower cost jobs for clients who I'm very interested in working with but who may not have a strong budget (e.g., nonprofits that are doing important things)," says freelance communications consultant Kate Henne. "In those cases, though, I always outline up front what my usual costs are, and in the invoicing I reflect a discount. That sets expectations for future work, not only with that client but with those they might recommend your work to."

A handful of freebies or discount projects is plenty to kick-start a skimpy portfolio, so don't even think about slashing your rates as a long-term marketing strategy. Underbidding your competitors by 50 percent to snag more gigs degrades your profession: You reinforce those cheapskate clients hell-bent on hiring writers, illustrators, and virtual assistants for a song even though they have the budget, and you wind up toiling twice as much to make the same amount of money. Or you wind up "giving them what they paid for"—a hastily slapped-together product you're not even proud to put in your portfolio—because you had to work at warp speed to make ends meet. We'll talk more on how to negotiate a project rate in the next chapter, though.

Paid Ways to Sneak Through a Client's Back Door

When you're trying to wedge a foot in the door as the low freelancer on the totem pole, giving it up for free (or cheap) isn't your only option.

Remember being a fresh-faced admin assistant back in your early cubicle-monkey days? And remember how you initially had to take on a couple of crappy projects no one else in the office would do so you could win over the big cheese? The same good old-fashioned dues-paying works like a charm in the freelance world too.

Here's an example: Suppose a women's clothing boutique from your Top Ten client list hires a freelance stylist to design and install their annual Valentine's Day window display. Now suppose that freelance stylist delivers the design specs but has a tiff with the store's creative director and bails on the project before installing it. Frantic to get the window finished, the creative director remembers that charming letter of introduction a budding freelance stylist (for the sake of argument, you) emailed her last week. Within minutes, she's on the phone with you, asking if you can help paint, light, and install the display the next day.

Cut to your office, where you're jumping out of your chair, pumping your fist in the air, and silently mouthing, "Fuck yeah!" You tell the creative director you'd love to help out, provided you can clear your schedule. (You don't want to give the impression that you have nothing better to do—even if you don't.) As your client-to-be is apologetic about the last-minuteness of the gig, you don't make a big stink about it. And although you'd have preferred being hired to design and acquire props for the display too, you don't turn up your nose at this production gig that's landed in your lap. You know a good investment of your time when you see one. If you show up on time tomorrow and paint like a superhero, the bigger, better gigs for this client will be right around the corner.

In my early freelance years, I had no qualms taking a project that wasn't necessarily my first choice if it was for a client I coveted. I'd write a piddly two-hundred-word gadget review for an in-flight magazine knowing a job well done could lead to a beefier feature story next time or the time after that. I'd agree to proofread a book manuscript knowing I could probably convince the publisher to hire me to copyedit a gig or two down the line. I even took a couple of "We need it by 8:00 AM

Monday morning—sharp!" copywriting jobs assigned to me at 4:30 PM on a Friday to get in good with a hotshot high-tech client.

There's no law against double-dipping—freelancing for more than one person or department at an organization—provided your clients don't mind sharing. (The last thing you want is coworkers fighting over who "gets you" first—awkward!) I've simultaneously edited manuscripts and written book cover copy for a couple of the technical publishers I've freelanced for. Either one department would recommend me to another, or I'd wait till I'd earned a client's undying love and then ask for an introduction to another manager or department at the company (another way to sneak through the back door!). As long as my deadlines for different managers didn't conflict and I didn't ditch my first contact, my clients were happy to pass me around the office.

When it comes to doing a stepping stone gig or two for a dream client, you have my permission to throw those project minimums we talked about in Chapter 8 out the window. So you don't get pigeonholed, gently remind the client that you're not only a whiz at window display production, you're a crackerjack at retail window planning and design, with the portfolio to prove it. And if you get offered a rush job or a job outside your normal business hours, be sure to let the client know that in the interest of getting acquainted with them, you're happy to accommodate them this once—at no extra charge—but that you normally require a rush fee (something we'll talk more about in Chapter 14). Then make sure your invoice shows that you waived the rush charge so the client knows what to expect next time.

Don't be afraid to push beyond your comfort zone if a dream client invites you aboard a project that's a bit outside your area of expertise but one you know you can handle. This is what's known as a lucky break. My first few years in business, when a potential client asked "Have you written case studies before?" I usually would say, "Yeah, but only once or twice, and that was just for a friend." Realizing this was not the preferred answer—and that software case studies weren't much of a stretch from the marketing docs I'd been writing—I began leaving it at "yes" and showing off my one or two relevant samples as though they were the pick of the litter. As long as I had a reference book I could consult (*The Chicago Manual of Style,* the *Microsoft Manual of Style for Technical Publications,* et cetera), a seasoned freelance friend I could go to with questions, and a sample of how the completed project was supposed to look, I was happy to take the leap.

Good Spec, Bad Spec

A client asks you to design a couple of logos for her consulting firm, saying she'll pick the best one. Maybe. If there's one she likes. Only then will you receive a contract and compensation for your work. Otherwise, no guarantees; you could wind up doing the work for nothing. This is what's known as working on spec, and it's something you should run far, far away from.

"Nothing I've done on spec has ever paid off," says illustrator Molly Crabapple. "My mother, an illustrator for thirty years, has also never seen a dime from her many instances of spec work."

That said, when you move from the commercial to the creative realm, it's a whole different ballgame. The "create now, hopefully sell the piece and collect a couple bucks later" model is the nature of the business. If you're an unknown novelist in search of a book deal, you have to write the whole book first before you can sell it to a publisher—and even then there are no guarantees you'll be able to find a buyer. If it's a record deal you want, you have to record a demo CD first. If you want to publish a specific essay, cartoon, or photo in a magazine you don't yet have a relationship with and you're anything less than a household name, you also need to create the piece first; it's unlikely an editor will commission it sight unseen. Freelance journalists, too, must pitch their nonfiction article ideas (not to mention book ideas) to the editors who already know and love them—again, with no guarantees.

I've submitted the infrequent essay or humor piece on spec to legit lit journals, anthologies, and big-name media outlets over the years with about

⇨

⇨

a 60 to 70 percent success rate. Even if you don't publish or sell the piece right away, you're building up your creative portfolio. Keep at it for a couple years, and you just might amass a CD's worth of songs, a gallery exhibit's worth of paintings, or a book's worth of poems.

If you're not sure whether spec work is SOP for a market or industry you're trying to crack, do your homework. Read the industry rags. Talk to other freelancers who've been there and pitched that. Visit the websites of the leading professional associations in the field. Because your time is a terrible thing to waste.

That said, if you're utterly devoid of the necessary skills, faking it till you make it is a recipe for disaster. If you've never picked up a camera in your life, don't embarrass yourself by accepting a commercial cinematography gig. One of my most painful gigs in the younger, stupider era of my freelance career was writing a script for a videotape that came with an anti-aging cream some fading soap opera star was hawking on an infomercial. Because I'd once faked my way through cowriting a crappy screenplay with a friend, I convinced myself I could handle writing a sixty-page commercial script. Because the video producer was perpetually drunk, she believed me. To say that I had no idea what I was doing would be generous. My script was incoherent at best, and the producer wound up rewriting every line. Needless to say, I wasn't asked back to that party.

Paid in Exposure: Slice of Heaven or Pie in the Face?

Here's my most hated statement in the freelance lexicon: "We can't pay you, but think of all the exposure you'll get!"

Throughout my freelance career, I've been offered almost as much "paid in exposure" creative work—what I like to call PIE—as work that pays an actual living wage. And let me tell you, at this point in my career the offers of PIE are starting to get a bit stale.

"Too often, some guy with an 'idea' and 'connections' will want you to do lots of free work, promising you riches later. He's lying. If he really believed his idea was going to take off, he'd invest his own money in it," Molly says.

But for every shady guy with questionable "connections," there's a reputable webzine, literary journal, art gallery, or rock club with shallow pockets that's put many a green freelancer on the map. And when you're new to the writing, performing, or visual arts table, a big helping of PIE can feed your career for weeks, even months, to come.

"When you're first starting out, that's what you want," says cartoonist, illustrator, and graphic novelist Ellen Forney. "You want to get your work out there, in as many places as possible, as many times as possible."

For example, I'll write the occasional article for an independently owned magazine I strongly believe in, despite the modest pay. What these magazines lack in budget, they make up for in visibility and portfolio pick-me-ups, so much so that their pages are often peppered with contributions by big-name writers, illustrators, and photographers. In fact, my previous book, *The Anti 9-to-5 Guide,* stemmed from an article I wrote for *BUST,* one of my all-time-favorite indie magazines. If that's not PIE, I don't know what is.

Of course, for every freebie or low-paying gig that *does* pay in exposure or portfolio boosts there are one hundred more PIE gigs that aren't worth the aluminum tin they came in. One telltale sign a PIE gig is half-baked: You and your growing posse of freelance friends have never heard of the outfit in question or anyone working for it. Another: The person offering you a slice of PIE doesn't have any written materials she can send you about the project or the size of its audience. Yet another: Googling doesn't turn up a website or any media coverage of the organization.

In fact, if someone goes out of their way to tell you they're paying you with PIE, they're probably trying to convince *themselves* they're offering you a sweet deal. Classy outfits don't need to tell you how great their gig will be for you; they know you're well aware of this fact. Some of my most hated "selling points" of these glorified volunteer positions:

- "You'll be first in line to get paid if and when we do start paying our freelancers. There may even be an opportunity for revenue sharing somewhere down the line." (Thanks for the, um, generous offer, but I think I'll just go work for some other no-name outfit that actually has a freelance budget.)
- "We'll credit you for your work and link to your website." (Here's a hint: Unless I'm ghostwriting, *all* my clients do this.)
- "You'll be an affiliate/web partner/paid per click on the articles, artwork, or photos you provide us." (In other words, you're too embarrassed to write me a check for five bucks, so you're masking the paltry pay with an elaborate yet worthless royalty scheme.)

When it comes to choosing your "exposure" projects wisely, novelist, journalist, and retired stand-up comic Lynn Harris serves up this reminder: "If you're going into something where creativity and work intersect, you can't let people take advantage of you. Because there's this prevailing notion of 'You're doing what you love—why do you need to get paid?'"

If you're hungry for recognition, grab a quick snack at the PIE counter of a reputable establishment. But don't gorge on empty calories. If you want the world to take you seriously as a creative professional, you need to start bringing home the bacon.

Chapter 11

Let's Make a Deal
How to negotiate project terms and rates you won't live to regret

"Just as you have trained yourself (or have been trained) to be a mouse, you can teach yourself to be a tiger (nonkilling variety)."

—Jean Baer, *How to Be an Assertive (Not Aggressive) Woman in Life, in Love, and On the Job: A Total Guide to Self-assertiveness*, 1976

Let's get one thing straight: Negotiating your price with a client won't turn you into Gordon "Greed Is Good" Gekko, the Michael Douglas character in the movie *Wall Street*. And yet, too many freelancers fear negotiation like a root canal, to the point that they're willing to accept any offer a client makes, no matter how rotten.

"I'm not the kind of person who plays hardball," the negotiation-phobes will say. "I feel bad asking for more. What if my client gets mad at me?"

Contrary to what a handful of professors studying society's perceptions of female mice who ask for a little extra cheese would have us think, your clients won't dump you for standing up for yourself. They may say, "I'm sorry, I can't go any higher." But unless you behave like a total ass, they'll still hire you. After all, a talented freelancer in the hand is worth two hundred unread resumes in the bush.

Besides, this is your career, not a popularity contest. If you wanted new friends, you'd make a MySpace page or join a bowling league (rather than work at home alone in your bathrobe). So forget the retro notion that negotiating is rude, sleazy, or—god forbid!—unfeminine. Remind yourself that this is your rent money, your salary, your livelihood. Men have been asking for more compensation for decades and have lived to tell the tale. It's about time we women did the same.

Before You Do the Math, Do the Recon

In Chapter 9, I told you not to price a project until you have all the details. I'm going to assume you've already done the necessary detective work to ensure your client-to-be isn't the Bride of Chucky (if not, see "How to Spot a Hell Client at Twenty Paces" in Chapter 14). But before you start batting around numbers with the client, you also need to square away the following information:

- ☐ Who will be your go-to person for the project in case you have questions? (If not the contact you're talking to now, then who?)
- ☐ Who else will you be working with and in what capacity? (Who will get you all the photos and testimonials for the website you're being hired to build?)
- ☐ How many revisions will be required?
- ☐ Who will be reviewing your work and signing off on the final product?
- ☐ What type of feedback can you expect? (Is the main concern that you get the client's "voice" and branding right, or are the reviewers known for their heavy-handed markups?)
- ☐ What's the deadline for each stage of the project (first through final versions)?
- ☐ What's the copyright situation? (For many commercial jobs, the client will want all rights to your work. But when creating your own essay, song, or photo for publication, performance, or exhibition, you absolutely want to retain ownership. Much more on copyrights in Chapter 12.)

Be sure you get a handle on all the project contingencies that might require unusual or runaway expenses on your part: long-distance calls, shipping fees, travel costs, pricey supplies you don't normally use, equipment rental fees, and the like. Ask as many questions as you need to. Most clients won't spell everything out—their biggest concern is finding someone who can get the job done on time and under budget. It's up to you to connect the dots. (We'll talk about when and whether to bill for project expenses later in the chapter.)

How to Reign in Runaway Negotiations

Clients who don't know what they want can chew up countless hours of your time with exploratory emails, phone calls, meetings, and requests for more details, if you let them. Ditto for blood-sucking zombies who milk you for free advice but have no intention of ever hiring you. Here are some suggestions for "training" indecisive clients and weeding out the bloodsuckers:

CAP GETTING-TO-KNOW-ME MEETINGS. Bloodsuckers are fans of meetings with agendas like "let's spend the next four hours talking about how you'd execute our project were we to actually offer it to you." For this reason, I have a rule about complimentary getting-to-know-me meetings: One hour max is all you get—by bat phone, webcam, or in the flesh—and then I'm billing you for it. Likewise, I don't dress, drive, and give up my morning for just anyone. Unless there's big money, repeat business, or real PIE potential, I phone it in.

USE TEMPLATES. Although I have a bio and work samples on my website, I still need to email interested clients my references, additional samples, and a more detailed bio or resume from time to time. The materials I send vary wildly, depending on whether I'm talking to an arts organization that wants me to teach, a potential copywriting client, or a news website that wants an article written. Rather than reinvent the wheel each time, I have a nice collection of templates I employ: ShamelessInstructorPromo.doc, Fortune500Bait.doc, and MediaWhore.doc.

CREATE A FAQ. Rather than answering the same questions over and over, email a "How I Work" doc to interested clients. Or post an FAQ page on your website, as mentioned in Chapter 5. "Before I do any illustrations, I send clients a detailed breakdown of how I work, how many sketches I do, what

⇨

⇨

sorts of changes they can ask for, and when payment is due," says Molly Crabapple. "So many headaches averted!"

SEND A QUESTIONNAIRE. Besides having a helpful FAQ and Design Process page on her company's site, Emily Carlin of Swank Web Style cuts to the chase by sending a design brief for interested clients to fill out. We're talking twenty-plus questions about everything from the site's purpose and number of pages to preferred colors, graphics, and layout. Considering how many people will call a web designer before they have any idea what they want, this saves her a load of time.

MAKE A VIDEO. For Erin Blaskie, who runs Business Services, ETC, a virtual assistance company based in Ontario, Canada, creating a ten-minute video called "How to Work with a Virtual Assistant" was "the smartest thing I've ever done." Not only has it greatly reduced the time she spends answering potential clients' questions about how she works, it adds a personal touch. "What's nice about the video is instead of it being written, they get to see who I am," she says. "It's a great way to get that trust built."

Do have a business-savvy pal in your industry weigh in on any FAQs, web pages, or videos you make before you send them to potential clients, especially if you're new at this. You don't want to be so demanding—"Only green M&M's in my dressing room!"—that no one wants to hire you.

If you find any of your client's expectations about the work process unreasonable, now's the time to speak up. Behold: "I appreciate that each of the thirteen people on your team would like to weigh in with their individual commentary on my first pass. But I normally work with one person on project revisions. I've found that having one contact who consolidates all feedback before passing it along to me helps keep the project on schedule and on budget."

Position it as a time and money saver for them, and they'll read you loud and clear. Remember, the client is hiring you because you're the expert. Don't be afraid to act like one.

Cozy Up to Your Calculator

Once you have the skinny on what the job entails, it's time to hunker down with your calculator and price the project. I strongly recommend you tell the client you'll get back to them with a price later that afternoon or first thing the next morning rather than do the math with them on the phone. It's far too easy to underbid a job when you give a quote on the spot. In your haste, there's a decent chance you'll forget to factor in the weekly check-in meetings the client wants, or the hundreds of dollars in shipping costs the project will run you.

Your first task is to plot out how long each piece of the project will take and add them up. I'm talking every meeting, phone call, email, Google search, outline or rough sketch, draft, revision, and final check you think you'll need to do. Now's not the time to be optimistic about how fast you think you can work; when in doubt, err on the "slow and steady" side.

If you've edited promotional videos, recorded podcasts, or translated books similar in topic and length to the project at hand, you of course should use those gigs as a guide to pricing the job on your plate today. Hopefully you tracked your hours on those past projects. (If not, there's no time like the present to start, something we'll talk about in Chapter 17.) And if you're utterly stumped as to how long a project might take you, ask your growing posse of freelance pals to weigh in. Believe me, this will become second nature before you know it.

Once you have your best estimate of how long the work will take, grab that hourly rate for your services that you determined back in Chapter 6 (not your break-even rate, but the rate that has you earning a pretty profit). To arrive at the project price, multiply your estimated hours for the project by your hourly rate. For example, $80 an hour x 30 hours = $2,400. As everything always takes longer than you think it will, pad that amount by at least 10 percent. So, using our example, $2,400 + ($2,400 x .10) = $2,640, which you might as well round up to $2,700. This is your bottom line, meaning unless there's serious PIE potential or you're up for giving a one-time friends-and-family discount, you're not going to do the work for less than this amount.

Before you go to the client, make sure this bottom line sits well with you. If $2,700 doesn't look like enough given all the project variables (tight deadlines, ultra-confusing subject matter), raise it to a rate you can live with. A friend of mine who ran a web hosting firm for eight years used to add a Headache Tax of 50 percent to any project he knew was going to be especially difficult (of course that's not the language he used with his clients). Since he wasn't willing to do the job for less, he didn't worry about the client balking at the price. And since the projects *were* more cumbersome, the clients usually went for it.

Taxi Meter vs. Limousine Rates

There's a lot of debate in the freelance community about whether it's best to quote a client an hourly rate or a flat project fee, the two most common ways we freelancers invoice. Thing is, one billing model does not fit all. I billed by the hour, day, week, month, word, page, and project before becoming the per-project gal I am today.

But let's talk about you. If you're a lawyer—notorious for taxi-meter rates—or someone who sells her services by appointment—cosmetologist, reflexologist, baby-sleep consultant—you'll likely charge by the hour. ("For $150 an hour, I come to your home and show you how to get your infant to fall asleep without treating you to forty-five minutes of blood-curdling screams." And if they protest: "All my clients pay this rate.")

Things get more nebulous, however, when you start to plan, code, draw, index, enact, promote, produce, or record something. Charge by the hour, and you risk being penalized for your experience, especially on small jobs you could do in your sleep. For instance, if a publicist can finish in ten hours what used to take her twenty hours to do three years ago, she shouldn't have to earn half as much now. If anything, she should bring home *more* bacon today given her growing PR savvy and media contacts.

And suppose that same plucky publicist has determined it's not worth her while to take the job for less than $2,500, even though it may only take her 10 hours to complete. Although her client may not bat an eye if she tells him "That'll cost you $2,500," there's a decent chance he'll gak on his decaf upon hearing "My rate is $250 an hour." To a client—whose compensation point of reference is the standard employee equation of $250 an hour x 40 hours a week = $10,000 a week = major rip-off—the flat limousine rate will sound far more reasonable.

Shall I Start a Tab for You? When and How to Bill for Expenses

Before you start a project, you need to consider any big, glaring out-of-pocket costs it might involve—that is, costs outside your normal day-to-day free-lance expenses. I wouldn't dream of asking a client to pay for a ream of paper and a printer cartridge, just as a makeup artist wouldn't charge for a couple bottles of foundation. Since these costs are part of our standard business overhead, we've already factored them into our base hourly rate (just like you did in Chapter 6). But ask me or that makeup artist to fly three thousand miles to do an article or photo shoot and you can expect to see it on your bill.

If you're not sure which of the smaller project costs you should ask your client to cover, look once again to your industry colleagues for cues. "It is not customary in my business to charge for supplies like discs and batteries, but it is customary to charge for production expenses like travel and shipping," says public radio reporter and producer Phyllis Fletcher. "In general, clients accept and happily pay the charges."

You might be wondering if you should just bump up your rate to cover any out-of-the-ordinary but piddly project expenses—$25 dollars of international phone charges here, one FedEx package there—rather than ask the client to reimburse you for them and risk being shot down. Yes, building the added costs into your rate can be more efficient than charging the client for them separately. But if a project's expenses exceed $75, I prefer to charge for them separately, so the client knows precisely what she's paying for.

On the flip side, some projects last too dang long or have too volatile a schedule to risk quoting a flat fee. Underbid a three-month gig and you could lose thousands. But charge by the hour and you'll get paid for every second you work. Besides, when you dedicate multiple forty-hour weeks to one client (greatly reducing your need for weekly pavement pounding and nonbillable work), even a modest rate of $50 an hour can be a windfall.

Seattle animator and interactive developer Rachel Bachman, who predominantly works on four- to eight-week projects with what she calls "crazy monkey deadlines," prefers billing by the hour. If you worked for her unpredictable software industry clients, you would too: "They leave my part of the job until the very, very end of a project cycle, and pretty much everyone else misses their deadlines and I end up in a tight, tight time frame—with some launch or conference set in stone that can't be missed," she explains.

In other words, since you have no idea whether you're coming or going, dear client, show me the hourly money.

If your client is skittish about paying you by the hour, give them an estimate of how many hours you expect the project to take. Or agree to cap the number of hours you'll spend on the project. Also let the client know you'll give them a heads-up as you near the estimate or cap. That way, your client can decide whether they want to trim some tasks from the work they hired you to do (so the price doesn't exceed the cap) or to forge ahead (paying you for every hour you work beyond the estimate).

The Trouble with Retainers

Ongoing projects for star clients make the freelance world go 'round. Show me a dream client who needs two $1,000 articles from me a month—that is, articles that earn me $75 an hour and up—and I'll show you a freelancer who saves herself many hours of trolling for work each year.

But there's a big difference between agreeing to deliver a piece of a fixed scope and price to a client on the first and third Monday of each month (or reserving a half day of services for them) and agreeing to do $2,000 of yet-to-be-defined work for a client each month whenever they say jump.

The first option obviously lets you retain control of your schedule. You know how long each lunch you cater or animated greeting card you create will take and what's involved with the job. The second holds your schedule hostage and can greatly reduce your hourly earnings.

How? Say you're a freelance web usability tester for WeHeart Widgets.com, which pays you a retainer of $2,000 a month in exchange for twenty to twenty-five hours of checking their site content, links, and downloads. Now say your friends at WeHeartWidgets.com send you the work piecemeal throughout the month—fifteen web pages to test here, thirty pages there—with your corrections to each batch due back to the We Heart Widgets mother ship within two to four business hours. Only you never know what day, hour, or week We Heart Widgets will be sending the next batch of web pages to review, as there's no set schedule. Plus, you're never sure how big each batch will be, making it difficult for you to schedule other time-sensitive projects during the month, much less stray from your email for any length of time.

Some freelancers would argue that such time-management gymnastics are a worthy trade-off for a $2,000 monthly retainer. I couldn't agree less. What the client is "buying" in this situation is someone who's on call forty-plus business hours a week. If you do the math (for example, 20 hours a month x 12 months a year = 240 hours / 52 weeks a year = 4.6 hours a week), you'll see that they're only paying you for an average of 4.6 to 5.8 hours of work a week. The only one getting a great deal here is the client.

The easiest remedy is to set some ground rules with the client about scheduling and deadlines. If this was my gig (and I have done a smidge of web testing on projects past), I'd insist on a setup like the following:

- Each Monday morning, the client sends me all web pages to be tested that week. I have till end of day Friday to test the week's pages.

- On the first of the month, the client sends me an estimate of how many web pages they'll need me to test that month, with a breakdown of how many I can expect each Monday.

- The client promises not to send more than 30 percent of the month's work on any given week. That way, I don't have to worry about receiving 75 percent of, say, February's work during the last week of that month.

- The client pays me $2,000 each month regardless of whether they provide me with the full twenty to twenty-five hours of work for the month.

- If the monthly workload the client wants me to do exceeds twenty-five hours, they pay for each additional hour of work (that is, if I have the time to take it on).

The idea is to "train" the client to gain control of their own production schedule so they stop monkeying with yours. Never sell yourself short by agreeing to on-call contracts. Get paid for each hour your client "reserves" you for.

The Master Haggler

So you've figured out your bottom line—the flat fee or hourly rate you want for the project and which, if any, expenses you need reimbursed. Now what?

Before you contact the client, get out your calculator one more time and pad the price (but not the expenses) by 20 percent. That way if the client tries to haggle you down, you have a better chance of getting the price you want. So if your bottom line is $2,500, the price you'd quote the client is $2,500 + ($2,500 x .20) = $3,000.

When you're ready to wheel and deal, phone the client and tell them you're looking forward to working with them, psyched about the project, and so forth. Be charming, but don't gush too much. Then matter-of-factly lay the numbers on them: "My price for a project of this scope is $3,000." Period. Be firm, yet polite. Skip the caveats or sob stories about your bloated Visa bill. Keep the fact that you've padded your bottom line to yourself. None of this will help your case.

Once a client becomes a repeat customer, ditch the 20 percent markup trick. You don't want to become known as a habitual bluffer with them. Pretty much defeats the purpose of bluffing, eh?

In a perfect world, your client will reply, "Deal! I'll email you a contract this week." But it's just as likely they'll try to haggle you down, either because they're trying to save a few bucks (despite having the funds) or there's no way they can afford your rate.

In the first scenario, the client might make a counteroffer like "I was hoping for something a little closer to $2,000. Would you be willing to come down in price?" Note the wishy-washy wording, a sure sign the client has some wiggle room in their budget. In this case, ask them to meet you halfway at $2,500 (conveniently your bottom line) and say that's as low as you can go—end of story. If, however, a client genuinely doesn't have the funds, they'll probably shut you down with a firm "I'm sorry—$2,000 is the max our budget will allow." Here, there's not much chance you'll get them to come up significantly in price.

For some clients, the rates are the rates are the rates, no matter what. You may want $3,000 to write that 1,500-word magazine feature or provide the accompanying artwork, but if the publication doesn't even have the budget to pay its star writers, illustrators, and photographers anything above $1,500 for the job, good luck trying to get your $3,000. Try to negotiate, yes. But know that you won't always win.

The good news is that money isn't your only bargaining chip. If a client can only offer you $2,000 for a job you think is worth $2,500 minimum, tell them "This is what I can do for $2,000," and suggest dropping a task from the project description, such as including a sidebar or reader survey with the article you're writing or interviewing DJs and caterers for a launch party you're planning. Or suggest shrinking the project by cutting the proposed three rounds of revisions to two or trimming a two-hour photo shoot to ninety minutes. Or ask the client to extend or stagger the deadline (hey, time is money!), allow you to retain your copyrights (more on this in the next chapter), throw in some swag (free merch or tickets), or anything else you can think of.

If you're signing up for ongoing work—perhaps to deliver one cartoon a month—you can also suggest a three- to six-month trial period at the price of $2,000 per piece, after which time you and the client will revisit the contract terms. (Be sure your contract mentions this trial period, though.)

As an alternate strategy, you might insist the client show her hand first, by asking what the project budget is right off the bat. "I did this on one of my first art jobs out of college. I was fully prepared to do the illustrations for $100 each, but held my tongue and ended up getting $800 a pop instead," says illustrator Molly Crabapple. If the budget is lower than your bottom line, tell the client you can't do the job for less than your bare-minimum amount and, if you need to, suggest ways to trim the project scope.

Whatever you do, avoid giving a price range when negotiating project fees. Think about it: If a shopkeeper tells you she'd like $60 to $75 for that cute sweater in the window, are you really going to pony up the full $75? Clients will go for the low end of the range every time.

Steer clear of the nickel-and-dime game too. There's looking out for your bank account, and then there's chintzy. I still laugh about the client who countered my proposed rate of $1.50 a word with "How about $1.45 a word?" Since we were talking about a one-time 2,000-word article, he was essentially trying to talk me down from a price of $3,000 to $2,900. If he really couldn't afford the $3,000, I suspect he would have countered with something significantly lower, like $2,500 or $2,000. If you propose a price of $3,000 and your client counters with an offer of $2,800, I'd seal the deal (remember, your bottom line is really $2,500) rather than return with "How about $2,900?"

As nerve-racking as it might seem, I suggest you negotiate by phone or webcam whenever possible. Email, IM, and text messages leave too much room for misinterpretation. Besides, people have a tougher time playing the hardass when they're talking to you face-to-face or by phone.

Before you agree to a job that's below your bottom line, remember that the price you accept now will affect all future negotiations with the client. It's much easier to negotiate up to the $85 hourly rate you'd wanted from $80/hour than from $70/hour. If you're not sure you can live with the client's final offer, there's nothing wrong with saying you'll get them an answer in the morning. For this reason, I love late afternoon negotiations.

If come sunrise the deal isn't sitting well with you, you have my permission to lace up your walking shoes. Like I said in Chapter 8, twenty hours spent on a gig you don't feel good about is twenty hours you could have spent looking for or working on a better project. If, however, like a tiger (of the nonkilling variety), you're ready to pounce on the client's offer, your next step is to get the agreement in writing—conveniently the topic of the next chapter.

Chapter 12

Get It in Writing
(but Don't Sign Blindly)
How to make sure your contracts don't suck

"A verbal agreement isn't worth the paper it's written on."

—Louis B. Mayer

A million years ago, I did a freelance writing job for a quasi-notorious self-help guru who shall remain nameless. I agreed to adapt a book she'd published into a script for an audiotape she wanted to record and sell (this was back in the Stone Age, before CDs). We didn't sign a contract. Instead, we agreed—on a handshake—to a price, a rough outline for the script, and when I'd get paid.

I thought I was pretty clever, asking for half my fee up front and half upon delivery of the completed project. Only I neglected to specify an appalling amount of crucial details, chief among them how many revisions I'd allow, what exactly constituted a "revision," and a project end date (in this case, it was the client who needed a deadline).

I'm sure you can see where this is going: Demanding client couldn't make up her mind about what she wanted the script to say and called for umpteen revisions, several of which could have been more aptly described as out-and-out fresh starts. Hapless freelancer stuck out the project for weeks after she'd anticipated finishing because she (a) had a misguided, almost psychotic need to please her client and (b) couldn't recoup the rest of her fee until the project was "complete" (whatever that meant).

I can't remember which one of us walked off the project first, or whether I ever recouped the second half of my fee. But I'm pretty sure I wound up making .04 cents an hour on that gig.

Without a crystal clear contract, you could find yourself in a similar time-sucking, money-losing situation. Even if your client comes highly recommended (my quasi-notorious self-help guru did), it's critical that you put every possible contingency of the project in writing. Because when things don't go according to plan—and if there's one constant in the freelance world, it's that things don't always go as planned—you'll want a signed piece of paper that proves what you promised to do, what you'll get in return, and what happens if the proverbial doo hits the fan. That way, if the worst happens and you need to take legal action, you'll have a leg to stand on.

As you know, I'm not a lawyer. And while I can share the highlights of what I've learned over the years about how to draw up and decipher a freelance contract, nothing replaces the counsel of an adept attorney who routinely works with artists, writers, performers, and other free-lancers. Likewise, I can't cover every possible contingency of freelance contracts in one little chapter. So use this chapter and the resources mentioned in it as a starting place, and then get yourself whatever legal help you need, okay?

Your Contract or Mine?

If you're freelancing for individuals or small organizations that don't usually outsource, you'll probably need to provide your own contract. The good news about writing a contract from scratch is that you get to start with a document that's 100 percent fair to you, the freelancer, which isn't necessarily what happens when the client initiates the con-tract. The bad news about writing a contract from scratch is that you have to write a contract from scratch, which, unless you went to law school or have created your own contracts before, can be a lot like trying to write an email in Sanskrit.

Hiring an intellectual property or contracts lawyer to draw up a base contract that you'll use for all your clients is your best bet. Yes, it may cost several hundred dollars an hour, but it can save you thousands of dollars and countless migraines in the long run. If you do go this route, be sure to get a recommendation from a freelance pal, and be sure to hire someone who has experience drafting freelance contracts. But if shelling out a minimum of $300 an hour sounds like a small fortune, fear not. I've listed several affordable options for legal aid in the sidebar on pages 126–127.

You have every reason to be alarmed if a client refuses to sign a contract. If they're not serious about starting the project or don't have the money to pay you, they have no business hiring you. And if they try to sell you on some lame excuse about being too busy to sign contracts or some hippie-dippy philosophy about the oppression of legal documents (both of which have happened to me), insist on a contract anyway. Tell them it's there to protect your relationship in case of disagreement. Offer to convert the doc to email, which, you might remind them, can conveniently be read on their BlackBerry. Or if they're one of those "allergic to legalese" sorts, use the word "harmony," and if they're really crunchy, the words "good energy." If they still balk, take your chakras and run.

When you freelance for megacorps and smaller firms that routinely outsource work, as I do, the client usually will want to send you their own boilerplate contract. These docs tend to be more formal and verbose, being that they're written by lawyers hired to protect the company's hide, sometimes (okay, often) at the expense of your own. Later in this chapter, we'll talk about some of the clauses to watch out for in these contracts.

Never blindly sign a contract a client sends you without reading it from start to finish. It's perfectly acceptable to take a few days to mull a contract over and consult with a legal adviser. If any terms you negotiated with your client before the contract arrived are missing, or if anything else raises your hackles (perhaps the client said you'd retain all copyrights but the contract says otherwise, as recently happened to me), now's the time to speak up. Like project rates, contracts are made to be negotiated.

A client who doesn't want to be bothered with contract negotiations may protest, "But this is the contract all our freelancers receive." (Even so, I'll bet it's not the one they all *sign*.) Or they might try, "This is just something Legal requires you to sign. It's just a formality. I don't even understand half of it myself." (I'll never see the logic in that argument, yet I hear it all the time.) Don't let any of this intimidate you. As with project price, you want to negotiate the most favorable contract you can from the get-go. Once you ink the deal, contracts aren't so easy to change, unless you're, say, Oprah.

Legal Advice That Won't Break the Bank

While I always thought it would be fun to bark "You'll be hearing from my lawyer!" I've never actually hired one. I've always been too, er, frugal. But that doesn't mean I've skimped on getting legal advice on the contracts I sign. If you too have a limited budget, consider these low-cost resources for getting legal assistance with your contracts. After all, some legal advice is better than none.

PROFESSIONAL ASSOCIATIONS. Organizations like the National Writers Union, Graphic Artists Guild, and American Society of Media Photographers offer legal advice and contract assistance to their members. (You have to pay to join.) But nonmembers can take advantage of the free contract advice on their websites.

LEGAL CLINICS. Services like Washington Lawyers for the Arts in Seattle, Volunteer Lawyers for the Arts in New York City, and St. Louis Volunteer Lawyers and Accountants for the Arts are a godsend. Not only do they

⇨

⇨

provide nominally priced legal aid, many offer low-cost seminars on contracts and copyrights. For a legal clinic near you, see StarvingArtistsLaw.com.

NOLO.COM. This website is a goldmine of free legal advice. Plus, it sells loads of affordable books and e-books on contract and copyright law—complete with contract templates!—including *Protect Your Artwork; Music Law: How to Run Your Band's Business;* and *The Copyright Handbook: What Every Writer Needs to Know.*

YOUR PERSONAL AND PROFESSIONAL NETWORK. I often compare contract notes with my freelance friends. And I'm not beyond asking my contract lawyer friend for the occasional quickie consult in exchange for a nice bottle of wine.

AGENTS, MANAGERS, AND ARTISTS' REPS. Besides helping you land shinier, better-paid acting roles, live gigs, book deals, or illustration work, agents, managers, and reps—who work on commission—can spot a crummy contract a mile away. Don't expect to find someone to rep you right out of the gate though; you need to be a creative superstar with a killer reel, demo CD, book proposal, or portfolio. For more resources on working with agents, consult a book like Michael Larsen's *How to Get a Literary Agent* or Tony Martinez's *An Agent Tells All* (for actors).

While I've relied on all the above to help me with my contracts over the years, I admit that the "cobbling together legal advice where you can get it" approach is wearing thin, now that I regularly need contract advice on my writing projects. What's more, professional and arts associations can't always grant you an appointment as soon as you need one. (My local legal clinic is only open a couple days a month.) For that reason, I've added "find an attorney" to my business infrastructure to-do list.

No-Frills Contract Checklist

Freelance contracts vary widely depending on the type of work you're doing and the size of the project. A contract doesn't have to be a ten-pound paperweight riddled with incomprehensible legalese. An informal one- or two-page letter often does the trick, as long as all the project contingencies are covered and you and the client both sign on the dotted line.

You can view sample contracts on KeepYourCopyrights.org and the websites of many professional organizations for creative freelancers (see the Resource Guide for a few of my favorites). And you can find contract templates for just about every type of freelance project in the books and e-books sold on Nolo.com. But since I don't want to keep you in suspense, here's a checklist of items your freelance contracts should include:

- ☐ Full name and contact info for you and the client (including company names)
- ☐ The date the contract will take effect—and expire
- ☐ A detailed description of the work you will do on the project, broken down by task
- ☐ The number of revisions you will do, meetings you will attend, status reports you will submit, and any other moving targets you can think of
- ☐ Dates you will deliver each milestone, draft, or version of the project
- ☐ A detailed description of the materials the client will provide and tasks they will do to keep the project on track (when they will get you the text they're hiring you to translate, give you feedback on deliverables, and so on)
- ☐ A list of any supplies, equipment, or office space the client will provide for you to complete the project, if applicable
- ☐ The fact that all tasks not mentioned in the contract will be considered outside the scope of the project and will require a new agreement between you and the client
- ☐ How much, in what manner, and when the client will pay you (by the hour or in bulk? at the start of the project, the end of it, in stages, or all at once? by check, direct deposit, or PayPal? and on what dates?)
- ☐ Which expenses the client will cover, if applicable
- ☐ Who owns the copyrights to the work you're creating (more on this later in the chapter)

- ☐ How you'll be credited for your work, if applicable (byline? bio? credit line?)
- ☐ Assurance that the client will run by you any changes made to your bylined or credited work before sending it to production
- ☐ How many copies you'll receive of the completed product
- ☐ The conditions under which you or the client can end the agreement (thirty days written notice required? client forfeits their project deposit if they cancel? client pays you for all hours worked prior to your receipt of the termination letter?)
- ☐ How disputes will be resolved if you and the client come to blows (arbitration? mediation? the state court system?)
- ☐ If you and your client live in different states, which state's laws will govern the contract
- ☐ A space at the end of the document for you and your client to sign and date

If you're the one creating the contract, send two signed copies for the client to sign too and have them return one to you. If your client initiates the contract, you may also see the following clauses, which are pretty standard:

- You're not an employee of the company (but an independent contractor), meaning you buy your own benefits and pay your own taxes
- The work you do for the client was created by you (as opposed to a subcontractor) and isn't owned by anyone else (say, another client you already sold the copyright to, or someone you decided to plagiarize)
- Any top-secret info your client tells you about their business dealings that you couldn't have learned from, say, Googling them is confidential and you pinky-swear to not blab it to anyone else while under contract with the client (what's known as a confidentiality agreement)

If your project start-date is rapidly approaching and you have yet to see a contract from the client, send them a letter of agreement—a brief, informal description of all the terms you negotiated with them. Even if you hashed out the terms of the project by email or IM, it's still best to put all the details into one doc or email so you avoid misunderstandings later. I have a few clients who are notorious for getting me the contract just as I'm wrapping up the project. But if I have a letter of agreement to refer back to in case anyone's confused about what I said I'd do, I won't sweat a stalled contract.

Own It! (a.k.a., When to Give Up Your Copyrights, and When to Clutch Them to Your Chest as Though Your Life Depended on It)

To a creative freelancer, retaining copyright ownership can be as important as getting paid a fair wage. If I sell an article, photo, or comic strip to my favorite indie women's magazine, you bet I want to retain as much ownership of my creation as I can. In doing so, not only do I have a say in where my work is distributed now and in the future, I have the option to make more money by reselling the piece to other clients or media outlets later—doubly important to me if the pay and PIE (exposure) I receive from the indie women's publication isn't much to write home about.

On the flip side, sometimes signing a contract that grants the client "all rights" to your story, song, or video or deems your creation a "work for hire"—in both cases, handing the client every last copyright to your creation—won't hurt you. If I'm doing a bread-and-butter job writing web copy about the latest and greatest database program my client's hawking or a radio jingle about a brand-new extra-plushy toilet paper product, I won't mind selling all rights to my work. For a corporate gig like this, I'd even expect it. It's not like I can resell those ditties anyway. And as long as the client's paying me handsomely, who am I to complain?

Unfortunately, countless print, web, TV, radio, film, and music empires try to extend these same rights-grabbing contracts to the freelancers they buy articles, broadcasts, scripts, songs, photos, videos, films, illustrations, and animations from. Besides having the right to edit or tweak your work without consulting you, when you fork over all copyrights to a media empire, they can distribute and resell your work anywhere they dang well please without paying you a cent. Hardly seems fair when some well-fed execs who stand to make a mint off your content—the guts of their media empires—are driving around in Jaguars and you're scraping to make rent.

"Some of those clauses can be so expansive, and suddenly you could find out, 'Wow, they've published this anthology through such-and-such publishing house, and now they're making all these royalties and I'm just sitting here with $150 I got for first publication,'" says attorney Michael Graham, board president of Washington Lawyers for the Arts. "You want to know where your work is going to end up and if you can keep it from winding up somewhere you may not want it."

Remember that the editor, producer, or art director offering you the contract probably didn't write it and may not even know what it says. If you explain your concerns, they may be willing to compromise. That said, don't request twenty-five nit-picky changes or drag out the negotiation process for half a dozen rounds. Clients only have so much patience. Pick your battles and have a bottom line in mind (you retain ownership of all electronic rights no matter what, client gets exclusive dibs on the piece for ninety days, et cetera). Then fight the good fight, make any necessary compromises (or walk from the project), and move on.

If a client who wants to buy your masterpiece sends you a rights-mongering contract, by all means try to negotiate a happy medium. A writer, photographer, or illustrator could push a magazine to buy only the first-publication rights to her work, meaning she can't sell the piece to anyone else first. Or she could press the publication to buy exclusive rights to the work for a specified period of time (three months, six months, whatever), meaning she can't resell the piece during that time frame. You could also try to limit the client to publishing or distributing your baby in certain mediums (for example, print but not electronic), or to prohibit the client from reselling your work (say, to a web partner or as part of a book anthology) without giving you a cut of the sale. The permutations abound.

I won't lie to you: It can be tough getting a corporate Goliath to bend to your will if you're not a household name. But that doesn't mean you shouldn't try. I'm inspired by Nikki McClure, who has corporations like Patagonia and Seventh Generation calling to license her images for their marketing materials for a limited period of time (meaning Nikki retains her copyrights). And I aspire to be more like Ellen Forney, whose choice to just say no to work-for-hire gigs enables her to publish books like *Lust,* a collection of illustrations she did for the adult personal ads in *The Stranger,* an alt-weekly paper in Seattle.

That said, if some high-profile media outlet dangles a well-paid gig with big PIE potential under your nose in exchange for a nonnegotiable work-for-hire contract, who am I to stop you? I've certainly taken the bait in the name of helping myself to a piece of the notoriety PIE, as have a number of freelancers mentioned in this book. Maybe you do a handful of pieces for some hotshot client to catapult your portfolio up five notches and then move on to bigger and fairer contracts. A freelancer's gotta do what a freelancer's gotta do.

So what's the big takeaway? Familiarize yourself with the copyrights issues and gotchas of your particular industry and trade. Become so contract-savvy that when you run across a clause deeming your creative masterpieces "the sole property" of your client "in perpetuity," not to mention "in any media, whether now known or hereafter devised," you speak up rather than blindly sign all your rights away.

Sites like Nolo.com, KeepYourCopyrights.org, and the online homes of creative arts associations—Recording Artists' Coalition, American Society of Journalists and Authors, and the like—offer loads of information, including explanations of troublesome copyright language commonly found in freelance contracts. And since copyright language is enough to make anyone's eyes cross, it's a good idea to get legal assistance. For low-cost resources, see the sidebar on pages 126–127 and the guide at the back of the book.

When Noncompete Clauses Attack

I understand why some companies like to put noncompete clauses—language prohibiting you from working for their competitors or their own clients—in their freelancer contracts. But that doesn't make me hate these clauses any less. No freelancer wants to sign away her ability to work for another company. If we wanted shackles, we'd still be someone else's employee.

That said, there are a number of valid reasons why a company might ask its freelancers to agree to a noncompete: They want to prevent you from sharing their trade secrets with a business rival. Their business revolves around product development, technical innovation, or fresh content, and they want to make sure the star freelancer they're hiring is giving them an "exclusive" on her ideas, inventions, or creations. Or, they've been burned in the past by freelancers poaching their clients and want to ensure this doesn't happen again.

Let's look at the exclusivity thing first. In some creative circles, it's taboo to get into bed with your clients' direct competitors. The editors I work with at my regional daily paper wouldn't take too kindly to me writing a story on a Pacific Northwest dog dancing convention for them *and* for one of the local alt weeklies. Editors don't want to be scooped by a rival, especially at the hands of one of their trusted freelancers. But that doesn't mean I can't sell a story on the same topic to a national media outlet or a publication in another region (like *Martha Stewart Living, The New York Times,* or CNN.com), as long as the story for my local client runs first.

If my regional paper is keeping me busy with a steady stream of assignments, I'm not going to mind that I can't shack up with their competitors. With any luck, I won't even have time to. But no way will I sign a contract saying that I won't write for their competitors for six months, one year, or however long into the future if my beloved paper and I part ways. (Then who would I work for?) Likewise, unless the money's really good, I'll have a hard time agreeing to a clause that says I won't sell an article about beekeeping to any other media outlet for the next six months. Instead, I always try to negotiate such noncompetes away, or at least down to a shorter time frame (for example, if the client wants six months' exclusivity, I'll suggest three).

As for agreeing to not poach the clients of a small agency or another freelancer who's subcontracting work to me, I'm happy to oblige—within reason. No one knows better than a freelancer that your clients are your livelihood. But if that agency or freelancer wants me to promise that after the project ends I won't work directly for their client for five entire years, I may try to get that time frame reduced to a year or two.

Plus, if an agency's noncompete would prevent me from working for a 25,000-person company, I'll want the clause narrowed so it only restricts me from working directly for the specific *department* the agency hired me to work with, not the entire company. Where I live, most technically inclined freelancers work for a certain 30,000-plus-employee software empire at some point during their career and have contacts throughout the company (yours truly included). No chance would I sign away my right to work with my existing contacts at said empire, though I have been asked to do so by a couple agencies with overreaching noncompete clauses in their contracts. I'm happy to let the agency keep their contacts, but only if I can keep mine.

Never Assume Anything

I know creating and negotiating contracts might sound more daunting than, say, performing oral surgery on yourself, but trust me, it gets much easier with practice. The most important thing to remember is that your contracts can never be too clear.

"Sometimes I think certain things are obvious, but then those assumptions come back to bite you in the butt," says writer/editor Ally Peltier. "For example, I just completed my first ghostwriting project. It was a heavily illustrated coffee-table-type book, something I've never worked on before. The publishing contract stipulates payment to be made in thirds: one third on signing, one on early delivery, and one on final delivery. Having worked in book publishing, I know this is standard, so I did not question it. However, when push came to shove, it turned out that the publisher considered 'final delivery' to include delivery of the final, retouched digital photo files from the book's photographer, something that would not occur until the last stages of production, which was more than six months after I sent in the manuscript!"

Ask any freelancer who's been nipped in the derriere by a contract with a nasty loophole like this and she'll say she made dang well sure it didn't happen again. Take West Coast wedding photographer Dani Weiss, who told me this tale: "A client postponed their wedding two times, causing me to lose work on both of the dates. They then proceeded to try and get their initial deposit returned to them. I ended up having to hire a lawyer to write a letter, which rementioned that my initial contract required a 50 percent deposit to hold the date. However, I ended up changing my contract to reflect a rescheduling fee in case this was to happen again."

Publicist Jocelyn Brandeis even includes a clause in her contracts stating what work she *won't* do on a project. "I've learned to put in my contracts several items that are not included in my services, so no one is surprised when I recommend outside services to help them," she says. Apparently a lot of PR clients expect their publicist to cover everything from their event catering expenses to their travel costs—go figure.

One last word to the wise: If a client tells you "Oh, that clause of the contract doesn't really mean what it says—I would never hold you to not working for our competitors" or "I don't think we need to update the contract—I'll remember later that I said we'd put your bio alongside each piece of your work," don't give in. What if your point of contact leaves the company and you're left without a written record of her promises? The legally binding agreement is the one you make in writing, not some off-the-cuff (potentially bullshit) assurance your client makes to get you to sign the contract.

Clear?

PART 3

Your So-Called Freelance Life

Part of the appeal of freelancing is that there's never a dull moment. With so many hats to wear, you can easily find yourself playing hired gun, customer service rep, and accounting manager all before lunch. On the downside—well, that is kind of the downside. With so many balls in the air and to-do's to keep track of, it can be tricky to stay in the black, focused on the deadlines at hand, and on top of your schedule (not to mention your shit).

That's where this section comes in. Consider this your guide to the day-to-day of keeping your freelance business humming along smoothly—without letting it overtake your personal life. I'll talk about the steps you can take to keep your star clients smiling, and how to deal with (and ultimately weed out) those hell clients who are all too happy to suck the time and life right out of you. I'll also cover how to keep your bank account flush, your ass insured, and the IRS off your back.

As mistress of your own schedule, it's all too easy to find yourself bouncing from urgent email to urgent email and lunch date to lunch date if you're not careful (meaning, no time for your actual billable work). To put the brakes on that train wreck, I'll discuss how to tame your unwieldy schedule, from banishing distractions and battling procrastination to hiring other freelancers and building time off into your calendar.

Finally, I'll wrap up the section with every freelancer's favorite topic: your master plan for world domination. Here, I'll offer up some suggestions for promoting your work with wild abandon and bringing home a bit more bacon in the process. Plus, I'll show you how to juggle the bread-and-butter projects that keep a roof over your head with the dream projects you really want to do.

Chapter 13

Care and Feeding of Your Clients

Stroke your customers and give them the happy ending

"Above all saleswomen, the one an intelligent customer is certain to like best—the one in fact to whom she always returns—is one who listens to what she says and tries to give her what she wants, instead of trying to sell her what the store seems eager to be rid of."

—Emily Post, *Etiquette: The Blue Book of Social Usage*, 1922

A couple years ago, while doing some prep work for a class I was teaching, I asked half a dozen clients of mine to lay their biggest freelancer peeves on me. A newspaper editor I adored coughed up this gem about a wannabe columnist who, lacking any comprehension of the word "no," hounded her via email for weeks: "Her last pitch to me said, 'I should have a column in the paper because, frankly, I deserve it.' This has now become a buzz phrase we use here to crack each other up . . . not where you want to be as a potential freelancer."

Ouch.

Fortunately, satisfying your clients can be boiled down to this tidy list:

- Remember that you've been hired to produce a product.
- Follow directions.
- Don't be a schmuck.

Simple, right? But you'd be surprised how many indie workers are ill-versed in keeping clients happy, evidenced by the tsunami of questions new freelancers ask their battle-tested counterparts. On the flip side, I've heard many a client grumble that it's hard to find good freelance help these days.

So how do you become the good freelance help that clients (and with any luck, all their colleagues) can't seem to get enough of? Since not following directions is one of the top client complaints, let's start there.

Say you agree to produce a straitlaced corporate website, some landscape design specs, or an investigative news piece based on the client's instructions. But somewhere along the way you get the idea that a neon green MySpace page, four-story tree house, or seventeen-page poem would be so much cooler than what the client had in mind. So you:

❶ stick a note about it in your idea file for future personal projects and carry on with the client project as planned.

❷ deliver two versions of the project: the one the client requested, and your "interpretation" of the assignment. With any luck, you'll get a bonus for your ingenuity.

❸ chuck the client's notes and do the project your way. After all, the talent knows best.

Obviously #1 is the way to go. Yet a staggering amount of freelancers try to turn in projects that are the wrong length, size, shape, color, angle, resolution, topic, style, font, or format. How do I know? Not only have I heard many client gripes on the matter, countless freelancers have asked me if loose interpretations of the required word count, subject matter, point of view, number of deliverables, color scheme, or software is okay.

I'm with Woody Allen on this one: Eighty percent of success is just showing up. That doesn't mean you should do a shoddy job. It means you should do *the job*—as in, the exact work your client is paying you to do. This includes but is not limited to the following:

- Taking notes so you remember the little details the client specified, like the fact that the bride does not want any photos of Uncle Stan splitting his pants on the dance floor.

- Checking your work for factual, grammatical, formatting, style, and other mistakes.
- Ensuring you don't leave any of the aforementioned proofing or cleanup work for your client.

"Here it is" are the three little words clients love to hear. No excuses. No caveats.

Capiche?

Can You Hear Me Now?

None of this is to say that clients don't want to hear from you if you have questions or suggestions, or if you hit any potholes along the way. Lisa Wogan, a former magazine editor in New York and Seattle who spent close to a decade working with freelance writers, copy editors, proofreaders, and photographers, likens freelancers with crappy communication skills to submarines. "You give them an assignment, and then they go deep and they're gone," she says. "Almost always, the submarines are the people with problems on their assignments."

As much as we freelancers like to think of ourselves as superheroes, we're not mind readers. Your client will appreciate any detective work you do on their products, competition, and corporate MO, but if you still have questions and you aren't entirely clear on what the client wants, it's your duty to ask, listen, and furiously note-take at the start of the assignment.

"You don't have to take a 'just give them what they want' approach. In fact, you're being paid for the skills you have and they don't," says Kate Henne, the former corporate marketing manager you met in Chapter 7 who spent fifteen years hiring many a freelance designer, web producer, and editorial type. "But you do need to listen, understand the audience and goals, and show how your work will deliver. Your client will appreciate lots of questions about the finished product, so don't hesitate to ask."

If I can't find a sample on the client's website of the type of article, white paper, or case study I've been hired to write, I'll ask the client for a link to a comparable piece they (or one of their competitors) published.

That way, there's a road map for us both. Some of my corporate clients even have templates they give their freelancers to follow. And if I'm in uncharted territory (new client, big-ass project, vague directions), I'll turn in an outline or a writing sample early in the project to make sure I'm on the right track. Same thing applies to editors, illustrators, and programmers: An editor might turn in a few marked up pages, an illustrator a rough sketch, a programmer a few snippets of code.

Don't underestimate the value of the check-in email. When you're working on a beefy, lengthy assignment, it's common courtesy to let your client know how it's going, even if you don't have any questions. "Don't wait to be asked every time," says Venture Architects managing director Melissa Krinzman, who hires freelance writers, researchers, graphic designers, financial analysts, and business strategists to work on the business plans her New York–based firm creates for its clients. "Establish the check-in point at the start of the project and stick to it. I like when the freelancer is proactive with me, rather than me chasing them down."

Since clients don't appreciate incommunicado freelancers, make yourself easy to reach. Return voice and email messages about active projects the same day, messages about new projects within twenty-four hours whenever possible. Use call forwarding and your mobile device of choice if you have to run an errand during business hours. If everyone on your client's team communicates about hot projects by IM, follow their lead. Clients don't look kindly on technical dinosaurs. As Wendy Merrill, founder of WAM Marketing Group, a virtual creative agency with employees and freelancers scattered across the country, says, "The freelancers who have really antiquated equipment and barely know how to fax—it doesn't work."

Unfortunately, some projects are riddled with curve balls. You might discover the logo colors the client wanted you to use are the same colors their top competitor uses. Or that all the nurseries in town are out of the Japanese maples your landscaping client had her heart set on. Or that a source your editor wanted you to interview for the article is vacationing in Fiji for the next three months. This is when what Melissa calls "the no-surprises rule" comes into play: Clients don't want to hear about these potholes the morning the project is due. Your best bet is to come up with a couple of alternatives for them to choose from and give them a call ASAP.

At the same time, try to remember that your clients are swamped. They don't have time to hold your hand and reply to twenty emails a day from you. "There are those freelancers who are vampires that require constant attention and care," says Lisa, the former magazine editor. "They want to take you to coffee and pitch you a lot of ideas, and the ideas are all bad, and they follow up too much. There is a really fine line between getting through to a client that you're there and available, and being annoying."

Ditch the Diva Act

At a recent panel I was on at my local university, an English Lit undergrad asked how often a freelance writer could expect to be edited: "I just don't want someone messing with my words, you know? They're *my* words."

I get the sentiment, but I also get that when a client is hiring me to write something—be it marketing copy or a magazine cover story—they have managers, customers, and policies of their own to abide by. So I do my best to work within those parameters. That means not throwing a temper tantrum when a client comes back to you with changes they need you to make. (We'll talk about how to put the kibosh on runaway revisions in Chapter 14.)

"Attitude is really important," says Wendy, owner of the virtual marketing agency. "Prima donnas, not so much. To feel that being brilliant is a creative license to be abusive doesn't fly. People are not necessarily going to remember how much something cost, but they are going to remember your attitude and how they felt when they went through the process with you."

That's not to say you should roll over if you don't agree with a suggested change. Remember, your client did hire you for your expertise. It just means you need to pick your battles. So maybe you prefer the word "the" to "these," or a green that looks more like aloe than a 1970s washing machine. Big whoop. But if your client is a diversity consulting firm and they're pushing for having a bunch of images of smiling white people all over their literature, it's worth going to bat for.

Likewise, if the piece has your byline or credit line on it (as opposed to being a commercial work for hire), by all means push back on any mistakes the editor, art director, or client makes. I once had an overly zealous editor add not only a dozen typos to a one-thousand-word article I'd written, but also a well-known Yogi Berra quote ("Baseball is 90 percent mental, the other half is physical"), which he attributed to my junior high school gym teacher. Not exactly one for the editorial hall of fame. Especially since my name was on the shutout.

Always be diplomatic with clients, no matter how frustrating things get. "You want to be really careful about not burning your bridges," says Lisa, the magazine editor turned freelance writer. "When every assignment is something you're selling yourself on, no one is obligated to use you. And there are so many other people out there doing the work."

In other words, even if you're swearing off the guy who almost cost you your writing career by falsifying quotes, don't get all Amy Winehouse on him and make a scene worthy of the tabloids. The freelance world is smaller than you think, and clients talk among themselves all the time. If you need to vent about a stupid client trick, do so with your freelance BFFs. To your clients, you should be nothing short of a Disney character, complete with chirping bluebirds, circling butterflies, and a crown woven from buttercups. I'm not saying you shouldn't hold your ground and have the firm, difficult discussions you may need to have about botched contracts and project curve balls. But remember that professionalism and diplomacy will get you much further than raging hissy fits.

Always Have a Plan B

Clients love resourceful freelancers who go the extra mile to ensure a project runs smoothly, or in the case of public radio reporter/producer Phyllis Fletcher, the extra one hundred feet:

> *"My first freelance job was for a radio network in another country that wanted an interview on the beach with an expert in stuff that washes up on beaches. I had to drive to a small coastal town, pull him away from a beachcombers' festival, provide a phone for him to be interviewed on, and tape him as he answered questions. This was the job that forced me to buy my first cell phone. I knew chances were good that the phone would not have reception, so my other purchase was one hundred feet of phone cord. After I confirmed that the cell phone didn't work on the beach, I went into the gent's hotel room, unplugged his phone, plugged the one-hundred-foot cable into the wall, tossed it outside, brought the phone downstairs to the beach, and plugged it in. My client called us, I rolled tape, and they got the interview with the beach sound they wanted."*

Needless to say, Phyllis's client was duly impressed by her clever contingency plan. Lesson learned: Think ahead. Exceed expectations. Then watch as clients eat out of the palm of your hand.

Leave Them Begging for More

The hope is that after one gig, your shiny new client will ask you back to the ball. But if an invitation doesn't appear to be forthcoming, don't wait for them to make the first move. For all they know, you're slammed with work or you're looking for a full-time staff gig. So when you're invoicing for your first completed project, tell your new client you've enjoyed working with them and you'd like an encore. Ask what their freelance needs look like over the next few months. Be calm, matter-of-fact; clients don't like the pushy car salesman approach.

If the client hasn't given you much feedback on your work, you can also add, "Let me know if there's anything you'd like me to do differently in the future." (Subtext: "I'm open to suggestions. Fire away.") Be prepared to take criticism graciously; don't argue or get defensive. If your client was on the fence about asking you back to the party, an opening like this might make the difference between her writing you off and her saying, "Your designs are gorgeous, but all those file-formatting mistakes you made cost us valuable production time. You need to get it together if you want this relationship to continue." At which point you should of course promise the moon (and make damned sure you deliver next time).

Once a client becomes a steady, it's up to you to check in with them every so often: monthly, quarterly, annually, whatever jibes with the size of your projects. (Notice how I didn't say every week—remember, clients love low maintenance!) Email them a quick, "Hey, I hope things are good with you. Your new website/issue/product looks really great—congrats! I'd love to work with you again and have some availability next month if you need help." More often than not, a steady client who loves your work will assign you a project within hours or days.

If a steady client invites you to a company picnic, a holiday party, or an in-house training on company processes and tools that interest you, by all means go (especially if there's free food involved). Ditto if your editor, art director, or manager invites you to lunch. Out of sight, out of mind. But get right under their nose, and you move to the front of the line for new assignments. Besides, face-time get-togethers can yield dishy insider details about upcoming product launches, budget cuts, personnel changes—all info you might not otherwise have access to.

Never lose sight of the fact that this is work, not play. When it comes to getting swackered, sharing the intimate details of your dating life, or discussing their ex-CEO's headline-making sex scandal, follow your client's lead. If they don't indulge, neither should you.

Time Waits for No Freelancer (a.k.a., How to Blow a Deadline Gracefully)

I waited till the end of the chapter to write this section because I was putting off admitting to you that I can't claim to have never missed a deadline. Every freelancer has her dirty little secrets; this is mine. And while I would never advise you to intentionally blow a deadline, I know how easy it is to paint yourself into a scheduling corner and need more time. So let's talk about how to avoid scheduling screw-ups in the first place, and what to do if despite your best caffeinated efforts, you find yourself woefully out of time.

Obviously ninja time management skills are in order. Tracking how long each project takes so you can better budget your time in the future is a must, as is getting to the bottom of any procrastination dragging you down (see Chapter 17 for tips).

As a rule, plan to have projects done at least twenty-four hours before the due date so you have a cushion for last-minute tweaks, fact checks, and email-delivery snafus. For beefy, multiweek gigs, give yourself a week's cushion. Don't fall into the trap of getting up superearly on the morning it's due to finish those last few hours of work. Take it from a recovering procrastinator: Not only will this make you tired and cranky and question why the heck you wanted to freelance in the first place, it will piss off your client when "I'll have it to you by 9:00 AM" quickly turns into "I'm sorry—it's now looking like it won't be ready till noon."

Familiarize yourself with a project's production schedule so you don't accept a deadline that's bumping up against your client's drop-dead date. Ask what will happen to your completed work—who's next in the assembly line, and what are *their* deadlines? Like freelancers, some clients are better than others at scheduling. If your manager, editor, or art director has only given herself a day to review your work and turn it around to her web producer, art department, or printer, pull your own deadline in by a few days. Better to have a smidge of breathing room, just in case.

Invest at least several months earning a client's trust before you attempt to use that get-out-of-jail-free card. Even then, only ask for an extension if you're giving the client plenty of warning (not the day it's due) and you know your client pads the schedule (see previous tip). If you do ask for an extension, don't launch into a long-winded sob story about your kid with whooping cough or another freelance project that's making your life a living hell; just say you're jammed up and ask if there's any leeway. Don't make this a habit, lest you get branded the freelancer who can't deliver.

Know that trying to change the game plan is a risk. Some clients are more rigid with deadlines than others, as evidenced by this warning from a friend of mine who works as a production manager at a creative agency in New York: "*Never* call me to ask for an extension of a deadline after you accept a project. That is the kiss of death. When people blow deadlines they are *off my list,* period." While this won't be the reaction of every client, consider yourself warned.

If you royally botch a project, fess up—never duck a client's calls. "Be honest, always. If you made a mistake, own it. Like anyone else, clients appreciate straightforwardness, and will more likely be forgiving if you are forthcoming and take responsibility for your errors instead of playing the blame game or making lame excuses," says Ally Peltier, who worked on staff as a book editor in New York for five years before turning freelance.

After you're pardoned (or read the riot act), don't dwell. Apologize once. If your late delivery made your client's life royally miserable, consider offering a small discount on the project fee or sending a gift certificate, box of chocolates, or a photo of a guilty-looking dog with its tail between its legs. Then chalk it up to experience, learn from your mistake, and move on. Sometimes the client will work with you again, sometimes they won't. But take it from someone who regretfully has committed this cardinal sin of freelancing on more than one occasion: One botched project or disgruntled client does not a washed-up freelance career make.

Chapter 14

The Client from Hell
What to do if a client stiffs you, moves the deadline, or otherwise bleeds you dry

"You're fired!"

—Donald Trump

B esides money and deadlines, what do freelancers bitch about the most? Nightmare clients. The scrooge who refuses to pay on time. The workaholic who starts texting you at 7:00 AM and doesn't let up till midnight. The creep with a crush who insists on dropping off the project specs at your house on a Saturday. The perpetually frazzled prospect who hands you the work three weeks late and expects you to turn the project around in forty-eight hours—over Labor Day weekend.

Most hell clients don't come with "666" tattooed on their forehead. At first blush, they may seem as harmless as a newborn puppy. Then, like the hand reaching out of the ground at the end of a third-rate slasher movie, they move in for the kill, sucking up your time, your money, and ultimately your soul.

Fortunately, a majority of terrifying client interactions can be nipped in the bud with clearer contracts and better boundaries. In this chapter, we'll look at several of the most common client maladies and some remedies for each of them.

PROBLEM: Your Check Is MIA

"For a corporate writing gig, I had the client actually come over to my house and bring me flowers in lieu of payment because they just couldn't get the money out of the company," says freelance writer and author Meghan Daum. "I was working from home doing this gig. But people who were working there had just stopped coming in because they could not get their checks cut. And I would call and call and call and the money wouldn't come. So finally the accounts person came to my house with a thing of flowers and said, 'I'm sorry.' It was just unreal."

Meghan's not alone in her tale of payment woe. Though we freelancers wouldn't stay in business for long if having clients stiff us were the rule rather than the exception, most of us have experienced the incredible-disappearing-check phenomenon at least once.

SOLUTION: Contrary to popular belief, when a client tells you "The check is in the mail" or "I sent your invoice to accounting weeks ago—you should have been paid by now," they usually mean it. In the past six months, I've had payments disappear into the void for an impressive array of seemingly innocent reasons: My invoice hit the client's email spam filter, the client had a personnel change in accounting and the new gal was backlogged, and so on. I even had a check arrive in an envelope stuck to the adhesive of another envelope that was addressed to—and contained a check for—another freelancer. Clearly an automation goof.

But what if it's not a quaint little assembly line goof? How can you protect yourself against clients who willingly hold your payment hostage for weeks on end, or worse, all of eternity? Some suggestions:

- Sniff out clients before you begin working with them to make sure they're on the up and up (see sidebar).
- Make friends with the accounts payable person so you can consult with them directly when a check's gone missing.
- For big projects, request 25 to 50 percent of your payment up front and have the client pay the remainder in chunks as you meet each milestone of the project (put all this in your con-

tract). If the client hijacks any of your payments, tell them you won't lift another finger until they pay up.

- Charge a late fee, something small, like 1 to 5 percent for every fifteen or thirty days the payment is overdue. While you may never see the late fee, adding one to your contracts and invoices can prompt the client to pay up. It can also annoy your star clients, so reserve this tactic for clients you're unsure of or pissed at.

- Hire a lawyer (or bribe a friend studying for the bar) to draft a nasty letter, as photographer Dani Weiss did (see Chapter 12). Here's where that written contract of everything you and the client agreed to comes in handy.

- If things get really bad, take your client to small claims court, which you don't need a lawyer to do. For details on how it works, how much it costs (not much), and how much you can sue for (usually just several thousand dollars, though amounts vary from state to state), Google "[your county] small claims court." There's no guarantee you'll get the money you're owed, even if you win your case, but sometimes the threat of court alone is enough to get a client to cough up the cash.

How to Spot a Hell Client at Twenty Paces

You wouldn't go on a date without first checking that your dining companion wasn't a serial killer, so why would you get into bed with a client without the same due diligence?

In Chapter 7, I talked about how befriending other freelancers and staying on top of industry news can point you toward freelance work. But it also can help you steer clear of nightmare clients. A quick email to your posse of freelance pals—"Has anyone worked with Seemingly Dreamy Client X? How was it? Anything I should be aware of?"—can spare you the migraine. Ditto for putting the same questions to an email discussion list you subscribe to. If I hear that another freelancer had to take a publication to small claims court to get paid—twice—I'll cross that so-called dream client off my Top Ten list in a heartbeat.

⇨

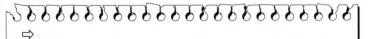

⇨

Other tip-offs that a one-time fantasy client isn't worth the shavings in your pencil sharpener:

- Your paper's business section or favorite industry website reports that they're filing for bankruptcy and no one's stepping up to bail them out.
- An industry site like WritersWeekly.com or GAG.org warns that they routinely stiff their freelancers.
- They have more employee turnover than the Gap.
- They're trying to liquidate all their assets, office equipment, and furniture via Craigslist.

If, however, you hear that a potential client is laying off staff, slashing operating budgets, relocating, or getting bought out, don't be so quick to write them off. Wait a couple months till the dust settles; people watching their coworkers lose their jobs may not want to deal with your inquiries at first, but after the storm, the company may find that they need additional freelance help to absorb the workload once handled by the people they let go. There's nothing shameful about inquiring.

On the flip side, if a star client you're already working with falls prey to a corporate shake-up, don't assume the worst. It doesn't always mean the freelance budget will vanish. I've seen dozens of clients grow, shrink, merge, and fall off the planet over the years (hello, nineties dot-coms!). And every so often, a new freelance job offer emerges from the rubble. So send a client in transition your good wishes, and gently ask if there's any way you can help. Get in on the ground floor of their reinvention phase and you just might find yourself rolling in work.

PROBLEM: Your Client Won't Stop Monkeying with the Deadline

Despite the contracts you carefully negotiate with your clients, scheduling delays, cancellations, and snafus do happen. Even if your client is a spreadsheet-loving type-A sort, she may have a disorganized boss, vendor, or customer who throws a wrench in her schedule, and thereby yours. If, as a result, a project you've "reserved time for" on your calendar gets held up by three weeks or is suddenly due two weeks earlier than you agreed to in the contract, you've got a problem. Ditto if the project now requires you to work when you'd otherwise be sleeping, vacationing, or attending your sister's wedding.

The last time this happened to me (okay, admittedly it was cutting into my vacationing and not a wedding—though I did once sneak off to finish an article during a rehearsal dinner), I thought I had only two options: (1) play the hero and save the day, even if it meant working overtime and skimping on sleep, or (2) point to the terms specified in the contract and hold firm, even if it meant losing the work. As I'd been trying to infiltrate the client for several months and was hot to prove myself on what sounded like a fun project, I chose—cue wrong-answer buzzer—door number one. What did this mean for me? That when the client sent me the two-hundred-page document they hired me to re-write on July 1 rather than on June 1 as they'd promised, I said "Sure, I can still do it." Never mind that I'd been twiddling my thumbs that June waiting for the job to come through and was already booked for another full-time freelance gig in July.

Stupidly, I convinced myself that caped crusaders worked till 4:00 AM and gave up their July (the one guaranteed sunny month in Seattle) in the name of climbing the freelance ladder. Equally naive, I'd signed a contract that didn't compensate me for such client delays. Meaning I *needed* to do the gig, however late, because I needed the money. Not surprisingly, I quickly came to resent the project and developed an out-of-control Red Bull habit, neither of which made me feel like much of a superhero.

SOLUTION: What I failed to realize at the time was that there was a third option. I could have remembered that the boss of my schedule is me, not my client. In exchange for me "reserving" all of June for my client, which required me to turn away other work, I should have insisted the contract compensate me financially for the reserved time, regardless of whether the work came through. Then it would have been easier to walk off a project I no longer had time to do.

If you can accommodate a client's jumping schedule without losing sleep, money, or your mind, go for it. But aside from being clear with clients on how much lead time you need for your work, what can you do to prevent crazy monkey deadlines from messing with your sanity and bank account?

- Charge a rush fee of 25 to 100 percent of the project price, depending on the hairiness of the schedule. What constitutes a "rush job" is up to you. For me, it's anything that requires me to work more than eight hours a day or over holidays and weekends.

- Specify a nonrefundable deposit in your contracts, applicable toward the project payment but yours to keep if the client cancels or reschedules the job. Depending on the work you do, this can vary widely. Piper Lauri Salogga, a Seattle-based interior designer, requires a deposit of $150 for her first appointment with a client, refundable only with forty-eight hours' advance notice. And if I were to do the aforementioned editing project from hell all over again, I'd want a nonrefundable deposit equal to at least a week's worth of pay ($1,000 for that project), refundable only with at least one week's notice of the project's spectacular delay.

- Make sure your contract specifies that you get paid upon turning in the work, regardless of whether the client uses it. (In the magazine writing world, writers sometimes find a "kill fee" clause in their contracts, which allows editors to nix our stories at will and compensate us with just 25 to 30 percent of the article fee. Needless to say, this isn't a popular clause among freelancers. If you stumble upon a similar clause, do your best to negotiate a 100 percent kill fee.)

- Help a steady client think about the bigger picture by suggesting you meet a couple times a year to map out the upcoming projects they'd like you to do. Yes, some of the timelines and assignments will change later, but this gets them accustomed to giving you more lead time (and hopefully more work).

- Consider hiring a subcontractor to help lighten your crazy monkey load. The client still gets the work done, and you get a cut of what your subcontractor makes (more on this in Chapter 17).

PROBLEM: Your Client Is a Bloodsucker

As mentioned in Chapter 13, we freelancers do extras for our star clients when we can: Float them an extra roll of film. Knead their backs for an extra five minutes if we don't have another client in the waiting room. Do a less-than-thrilling piecemeal project of theirs if they're in a jam and we have room in our schedule.

But there's a difference between doing someone a simple favor and letting ourselves be leeched. Some clients don't know how much time those "little favors" they're requesting take. ("I know we said we'd only have fifteen chapters for you to index, but can we sneak in five more at the same price?") However innocuous the request, if it's going to take you more than a few minutes or cost you significant coin, it's up to you to set the client straight. Sometimes all they need is a little schooling on how you work.

True bloodsuckers, however, cannot be trained. No matter what you say or do, they won't stop turning what should be a ten-minute check-in call into a ninety-minute bitchfest about their coworkers. They think you sleep with your BlackBerry under your pillow and have nothing better to do than answer their midnight missives. They repeatedly pump you for your "professional opinion" on any number of topics outside the scope of the project, from advice on how to redesign their website (even though they just hired you to write the copy) to advice on how to market their miniature dog sweaters (even though they only hired you to photograph them). In other words, they suck up a lot of extra time they're not paying you for, and they're happy to do it.

SOLUTION: I get that as females we're genetically programmed to try to make strangers like us and to nurture every last wayward soul on the planet. But try to remember that your clients are not your foster kids—they're just the people who sign your checks. It's up to you to draw the line in the sand. Some suggestions for dealing with needy clients:

- Tell them your business hours. (If you don't know what they are, see Chapter 17.) Remind them again. Then tell them you're not going to work for them anymore if they continue to call after your kids have gone to bed.

- Two words: caller ID. Even better, tell clients to email if they need you and that for nonurgent matters, it may be a few hours before they hear back. And whatever you do, don't give out your personal number, home address, or IM address.

- Ask clients to lump email requests into as few messages as possible so your inbox isn't crammed with subject lines like "One more thing," "Forgot to mention," and "Last email this afternoon—I promise!"

- To avoid scope creep, always look at source material the client sends you right away. If they give you ten pages' worth of copy and photos but the contract called for you to create a six-page website, put your foot down or renegotiate the deadline and payment.

- If a client wants your professional opinion on an extraneous professional matter (I get "Can you tell me how to get my book published?" a lot) and it's not something you can answer in five minutes, tell them you charge an hourly consulting fee for such advice.

- If despite all of the above, a client continues to try to leech off you, finish the job at hand, then cross them off your list. You don't need the money that bad.

PROBLEM: Your Client Has Set You Up to Fail

Because we freelancers fancy ourselves superheroes, we sometimes agree to projects with insurmountable problems. Sometimes we see the red flags going in; other times they don't come into focus until we're knee-deep in the project.

Betty, the freelance project manager you met in Chapter 3, told me about a doomed gig she took on recently, overseeing the production of a corporate video for a new client. Betty knew the production budget for the video was too small for the look her client wanted, but she thought she could get around it. "I tried to come up with a creative solution for the project, like an inventive, guerrilla, DIY approach," she said. "It ended up that they weren't happy with my approach, but they also didn't really have any ideas about how I should fix it because there wasn't any money. They were sort of stuck, and we were both really frustrated with each other."

SOLUTION: I'm not sure why clients outsource such doomed projects, but I suspect it has something to do with denial and the myth that free-lancers have some sort of magic wand we can wave à la Harry Potter to save a project from any giant, rabid, snarling three-headed dogs it involves.

In Betty's case, her client asked her to step aside from the project and paid her for her time. Betty was more than happy to leave the project, as she was fixing to quit it anyway. "It wasn't the end of my career," she said. "I didn't take it as a failure. I took it as a lesson to learn from. If you see a red flag, don't think that this is the one time that you can work around it. Really work hard to announce those red flags to the team that's hired you so that they know what you're up against. I sort of went into a vacuum and said 'I'm going to solve this myself,' and that didn't work."

As for Betty's client, trying to cut corners wound up costing them big time; they still had to finish the video in house, and they had to use their own money to do it, as they'd nearly exhausted their own client's budget. So how can you avoid getting caught up in a similar lose-lose situation?

- If you can't negotiate the time and resources you need to get the job done, turn down the project.
- If you're partway through the project and realize it's doomed, loop in the client immediately. It's not just your problem. Let them help you.
- If you and the client can't come up with a viable solution and you decide to leave the project, ensure you get paid for your time. All the more reason to have project cancellation fees and payment contingency plans in your contracts.

Do Try This at Home: See If Your Clients Make the Grade

Sometimes you need to stare the facts in the face to realize you have a troublesome client on your hands. Making a Client Report Card can help. Here's a list of what I grade my clients on:

- ☐ Pays well and on time
- ☐ Gives me repeat business and recommendations
- ☐ Gives reasonable lead time and deadlines
- ☐ Doesn't try to squeeze extra work out of me for the same price
- ☐ Communicates key information in a timely manner
- ☐ Doesn't need me to work from their office or come in for meetings
- ☐ Is pleasant and easy to work with
- ☐ Looks great on my bio (pays in prestige)
- ☐ Assigns creative, fun projects
- ☐ Gives my work great placement (on the home page of their website, on the front of the magazine cover, or as the leading lifestyle story in the Sunday paper)

I'm guessing "pays well and on time" ranks high on your list, too. But if you have other client characteristics that are important to you— for example, allows you to work as part of a team, or assigns projects that require you to travel—tailor this list to suit your own freelance needs. Then, using the traits listed on your Client Report Card as a guide, give each client you've worked with in the past year an overall grade: A, B, C, D, or F. (You can also evaluate future clients this way.) Maybe a client gives you loads of work, is wonderfully charming, and has recommended you to some of their colleagues. But since you've had to hunt down your check from them on multiple occasions, you give them a C.

Don't think that you have to play Donald and fire any client who earns less than an A or B. Before you go to extremes, tell the low achievers on your client roster that you love working with them, but you need more lead time, less scheduling snafus, a nonrefundable project deposit—whatever's important to you.

If that doesn't get you anywhere, send them packing. Remember, diplomacy is key. All you have to do to fire an unruly client is turn down the next job. However, if you want to do your part to help the freelance community, you can politely explain why. ("I can't hang with having to chase down my check every time.") Maybe if they hear it from enough freelancers, they'll get their act together.

Just as no freelancer is without her own charming quirks, no client can be impeccably organized 100 percent of the time. It's up to you to decide which minor inconveniences you can live with and which will make you break out in hives and default on your rent.

"Even when you're down-and-out financially, it never works to take on a red-flag client for monetary reasons," says graphic artist Colleen Lynn. "If you do, your situation will be worse in thirty days, not better. I will place my household rent on a credit card today and sweat out the 'lack of funds' situation before I take on a new client that may be a red flag."

I'm with Colleen: Given the choice between a nightmare client who's guaranteed to make me scream and a week or two of financial uncertainty, I'll take door number two every time.

Chapter 15

You're So Money

Tame your cash flow, save for retirement, and find insurance that won't bankrupt you

"Money is always dull, except when you haven't got any, and then it's terrifying."
—Sheila Bishop, *The House with Two Faces*, 1960

Y ou know my friend who sold magazine ads in Silicon Valley during the nineties dot-com boom, the one I mentioned a few chapters back? While most of my other twentysomething pals were struggling to make art and rent, Ms. Ad Sales was raking in six figures, playing the stock market, and decorating the spacious condo she'd just bought in one of San Francisco's spendiest neighborhoods.

Once, when I showed up at her Pottery Barn–perfect condo for dinner, she handed me her ATM card and PIN number and had me run to the nearest cash machine for her while she finished up a phone call with a client. Her checking account balance? Eight thousand dollars. *Eight thousand dollars.* It nearly knocked the wind out of me. At age twenty-seven, I was lucky if I had $800 in my checking account.

I remember being both awed and repulsed, not to mention a wee bit intimidated. *Who has that kind of money?* I thought. But as I'd come to realize by my thirtieth birthday, having enough money so you don't wake up at 3:00 AM panicking about the rent you were supposed to pay a week ago is incredibly liberating. It's much easier to focus on the projects on your plate when your mind's not crowded with panicky thoughts like *Holy crap! What am I going to dooooooooo?*

I'm not saying you need to have a six-figure investment portfolio or a home featured in *Architectural Digest* to ease your mind (lord knows, I don't). I'm saying that if you've been living with your head in the sand about how you're going to pay your bills each month, it's time to pull it out. Since freelancers don't get a nice, neat paycheck for the same amount every two weeks and we don't have an employer to chip in for our healthcare and retirement, we have to get militant about controlling our cash flow, lest we wind up back at the cube farm.

I can't go back in time and get my financial ass in gear sooner than I did, but I can tell you what I've learned since my twenties about making the sporadic freelance checks last throughout the year, finding halfway decent health insurance, and ensuring you don't have to spend your golden years living under the freeway.

Invoicing Is My Religion

Working for yourself means getting in touch with your inner bean counter—in other words, obsessively tracking your invoices and keeping squeaky clean financial records so you don't get dinged at tax time. (More on the latter in Chapter 16.)

Before I begin work with a new client, I ask when their accounting department cuts the freelance checks (on the 15th and last day of the month? Thirty days after receipt of invoice?), as this varies widely from company to company. That way I can be sure to submit my invoices during the soonest possible pay cycle. For ongoing work, I like to invoice once a month (less administrative work for me), but as long as your clients are up for it, there's no law that says you can't invoice weekly or biweekly. Again, this is something you should work out with your clients and factor into your contracts.

I haven't sent an invoice through the postal mail since the nineties; I use email. If it's a new client and they don't confirm receipt, I follow up to make sure they got my first invoice. I give every invoice I send a number (001, 002, et cetera—though you can use any numbering system you want). I've never actually had to use these numbers to reference an invoice later, but knowing they're there makes me feel more organized. To track my invoices, I use an Excel spreadsheet with these columns: client, project, fee, invoice number, date invoiced, date paid, and date I deposited the payment. I also divide the spreadsheet by quarters (January through March, and so on) and track the totals as I go, so I can see how my gross income's looking as the year progresses.

But my spreadsheet addiction doesn't stop there. Because I do dozens of projects a year, I keep another spreadsheet to track them all, using these columns: client, project, deadline, project notes, fee, and status (a.k.a., "in progress," "done," or "invoiced"). Not only does this show me what assignments I have due each week, it reminds me who I need to invoice. Anal, but so much easier than scrambling to figure out who I've billed and who I haven't.

Some freelancers use a program like QuickBooks to generate their invoices (and, I imagine, to automate everything I just described). I'm an old-school Word doc invoicer, though I keep a template handy so I don't have to reinvent the wheel every time. If you too want to make your invoices manually, here are the particulars you should include:

- ☐ The date
- ☐ The word "invoice" and the invoice number
- ☐ Your name, company name, and contact info
- ☐ Your client's name, company name, and contact info
- ☐ Description of the work performed, including date completed
- ☐ The amount owed, including number of hours worked and hourly rate if billing by the hour
- ☐ Any applicable late, rush, other fees
- ☐ Your social security or employer identification number (your client needs this for tax reasons, as you'll see in Chapter 16)
- ☐ The address where you want the payment sent (as I mentioned in Chapter 4, I use a PO box to keep my checks safe)

A word about getting paid: Call me old school, but I love being mailed a check. It's a nice affirmation that I'm actually making a living at this crazy boss-free life. (I still have the stub from my first book advance hanging in my office.) But armies of freelancers use electronic payment sites like PayPal and Google Checkout these days, especially those selling their services to individuals via the web (designers, virtual assistants, and business coaches) and those working in IT. If you go this route, make sure you read the fine print, boost your rates to cover any transaction fees involved, and see what other freelancers have to say about the service first.

Ebbs Are for Amateurs

Lots of advice targeted at new freelancers drones on about the feast-or-famine cycles of the independent professional's workload and all its maddening financial ebbs and flows. While it's true your workload (and thus, income) may vacillate between drizzle and shitstorm your first year or two, you should be working your heinie off to make those erratic ebbs and flows a distant memory as soon as humanly possible.

If you have a domestic partner or relative who's agreed to float you financially for a year while you get your freelance business off the ground, wonderful for you. However, thousands upon thousands of single freelancers bootstrap their businesses all by their lonesome year after year, yours truly included. So for the sake of argument, let's assume the only benefactor you have is you. In fact, even if you live in a two-income household, I suggest you pretend you don't. Fear of defaulting on your bills is an incredible motivator for drumming up clients in record time. Knowing your partner will pick up the pieces isn't.

Likewise, having a thousand dollars' worth of crap you can sell on eBay in a pinch will only get you so far. A better way to stabilize your cash flow is to build relationships with repeat customers who feed you a steady stream of work each month and pay swiftly. (For a refresher on drumming up clients, see Chapters 7 and 8.) That way, you greatly reduce your chances of falling into that old "Help, no one has paid me in six weeks and the rent is due!" trap we freelancers are so notorious for.

As you've seen in the past few chapters, despite the best-laid plans, projects can go horribly awry and freelance checks can go missing. That's why you need money in the bank, at least three to four months' living expenses, preferably six. (Personally, I start hyperventilating when my stash dips below the four-month mark.) I mentioned this in Chapter 2, but it bears repeating: Before you leave the 9-to-5 grind, stockpile as much coin as you can. If you've already made the leap to full-time freelancing and don't have much in the way of savings, cozy up to some of those less interesting, higher paying bread-and-butter gigs until you do.

Another way to combat the dreaded cash trickle is to stop spending the check before it arrives. "I don't think anything's real until the check is signed and cashed," says Stephanie Rabinowitz, a New York screenwriter and playwright who doubles as a publicist. "Ray Romano's production company can say they love my TV pilot, but until they give you money it doesn't count."

Once the check does come, an ongoing "don't access, don't spend" policy is a must. "I have a savings account with my regular bank, but it's too accessible," says business reporter Jane Hodges. "But if you shove your money into an account with an online bank like ING DIRECT, it takes a week to get it. I do this to control myself."

If your work is seasonal, become an income-rationing ninja (paging anyone who's ever tried to live off a book advance). Alisa Geller, who's worked as a freelance fitness trainer in Denver for fifteen years, sees a 50 percent dip in her client sessions each summer because, as she says, "Everyone is running and biking and Rollerblading outside. Lifting is just not their priority." But that's not to say she has trouble making ends meet during the warmer months. "I've never had problems paying my bills ever," she says. "The key is to just save as much money as you can in the winter. You take money from anyone, anytime, anywhere."

Because I'm foreclosure-averse, I like to take things one step further: I keep my favorite contract agency's number on speed dial in case every last client of mine goes belly-up and I need a three-month permalance gig to bail me out. While my freelance Armageddon fantasy isn't too likely, knowing I'm employable elsewhere helps me sleep at night.

Debit or Credit?

Sometimes I wish *Webster's* would just bite the bullet and list "frugal" as a synonym for "freelancing." After all, the ability to belt-tighten is one of the job requirements, something it took me six years of freelancing to get hip to.

Instead, I stupidly mistook my credit cards for cash in hand ("Why get a roommate to share my nine-hundred-square-foot apartment when I can just pay my rent with plastic?"). As a result, by the time I was thirty, my consumer debt exceeded my annual income. Between the seven credit card companies calling me round the clock for their money and the year's worth of back taxes—plus interest—I couldn't afford to pay the IRS, I was thirty grand in the hole. I found myself out of swipeable plastic, people to borrow money from, and the ability to live in denial for one more minute.

My accountant said I should declare bankruptcy; the powers that be would wipe the slate clean, and I'd be able to buy a house in about seven years if I wanted to. But my blasted bootstrapping gut would not stop screaming, *You made the mess, you clean it up.*

I'd like to think that all those tall tales of schlepping lunch pails and schoolbooks 150 miles across the suburban New Jersey tundra that my Depression-era grandparents told me had actually sunk in. But simple truth was, I felt like I'd flunked the grown-up test. You might as well have found me face down in a dark, dank alley, an empty bottle of Wild Turkey at my side,and puke in my hair. That's how rock-bottom I felt. And I knew the only way I was going to climb out of the gutter was to clean up my financial act.

Rather than bore you with all the gory details, suffice it to say I cut up my credit cards, consolidated my debt, and traded my footloose and spending-spree life in San Francisco for roommates and a ridiculously lucrative twelve-month contract at a software giant in Seattle. In other words, I sold everything that couldn't fit in my two-door hatchback, moved two states north, and embarked on a full-time permalance gig, complete with hour-long commute.

Yeah, I paid my debt to banking society, but between all the overtime and traffic snarls, it was hardly a joyous twelve months. And so I vowed never to fall off the living-beyond-my-means wagon again.

⇨

⇨

Now, any time I'm eyeing a pretty new laptop bag or a Balinese teak bookcase, I think twice before I swipe. I think about whether I'll be able to pay the bill off within the next few months, and whether the total interest I'll pay will cost more than the purchase itself. If my computer craps out and I don't have the cash to replace it, I think about taking on a higher paying, less interesting project to cover the cost. In the interest of staying solvent, I hope you'll do the same.

Retire in Style

Contrary to popular belief, freelancing does not equate selling your retirement down the river. Yes, you lose out on that employer-sponsored 401(k) and any corporate matching you once did or did not enjoy, depending on how generous your former employer's benefits package was. But thanks to a little something called an individual retirement account (a.k.a. IRA), you too can have a future that doesn't involve grazing on dog kibble.

There is a dizzying amount of IRAs to choose from, which you can learn more about on sites like Fool.com and SmartMoney.com. But the popular vote seems to be for the SEP IRA, which is easy to set up and, in 2008, lets you contribute up to 20 percent (or $46,000—as if!) of your annual pre-tax freelance income (you pay taxes when you take the money out at age fifty-nine and a half). Another winner is the Roth IRA, which let singles contribute up to $5,000 of post-tax freelance income in 2008 ($10,000 is the limit for couples; $6,000 per person is the limit if you're over fifty) and is tax-free on the back end. If you have the happy "misfortune" of having a six-figure income, you may not be eligible for a Roth IRA per IRS rules; check with IRS.gov or your tax preparer for details, as the income and contribution limits change annually.

You don't have to limit yourself to just one retirement account. "If you are gung-ho enough, the ideal is to fully fund your Roth and then max out your SEP IRA," say Manisha Thakor and Sharon Kedar, authors of *On My Own Two Feet: A Modern Girl's Guide to Personal Finance.* (I don't know about you, but I'm all for making that my next New Year's resolution.)

You can easily open an IRA with your favorite bank or investment firm. I suggest setting up the fund so your contributions are automatically withdrawn from your checking account each month. That way, you won't be tempted to cheat.

I had a money-savvy friend (okay, my mom) help me choose my IRA. But if it's professional advice you want, talk to a fee-only certified financial planner (one who doesn't work on commission). A number of them are willing to give you a one-hour, one-time meeting to help with retirement advice. As always, ask around for referrals. Failing that, see NAPFA.org to find a planner near you.

So how much should you save? "Self-employed or corporate-employed, the magic number for retirement is at least 10 percent of your gross income if you are in your twenties and thirties," say Manisha and Sharon. "If you are starting from ground zero in your forties, you'll want to target at least 15 percent of your gross income to retirement."

Do this even if you're making $15,000 a year as a freelancer. Seriously. I didn't start saving for my sixties until I was in my thirties, and I've been scrambling to catch up ever since—and not just with the money I contribute to the account, but in the interest I could have been making all these years if only I'd started sooner. Remember, the choice is yours: $350 cashmere sweater now, or dog kibble in your sixties.

Insure Your Ass

Over the past fifteen years, I've managed to rack up more health insurance plans than boyfriends, which I believe qualifies me to tell you a thing or two about spending several thousand dollars a year so that you don't have to spend ten times that amount should you get sick.

No matter how you slice it, finding and paying for health insurance as a self-employed person is a bitch. But so is trying to skate by without the coverage, only to fall on the ice, bust your tailbone, and wind up with an ER bill that eclipses your annual income. At the very least, you should cover your rear with catastrophic health insurance. Getting a more comprehensive plan with a high deductible ($1,500, $2,500, $5,000) is another way you can cut costs if you're reasonably healthy. So is skipping dental insurance (that is, if you have good teeth), which can cost more in annual premiums than just paying for your cleanings and x-rays out of pocket.

If you have the option to join a group plan through a part-time job or a contract job, seriously consider it. I've done this on several occasions through contract agencies offering coverage, and the plans were far more affordable than (and sometimes even superior to) going it alone. If you're leaving a staff job and have the option to sign up for COBRA coverage (eighteen months' continuation of the plan you had while on the job, only on your dime), make sure it's the best you can do, pricewise. Personally, I've never met a COBRA plan I could afford, let alone another freelancer who could afford one.

So where else can you find health insurance? Sites like HealthInsuranceInfo.net and AHIRC.org break down self-employed coverage options by state. If you're ready to buy, many freelancers swear by the comparison-shopping site eHealthInsurance.com. You can also find health plans through a number of professional associations, from local chambers of commerce to the Freelancers Union in New York (which at the time of this writing offered coverage in thirty-one states) to industry-specific groups like Mediabistro, Graphic Artists Guild, and Professional Photographers of America.

The last time I needed a new insurance plan (after finishing a contract gig that had given me health coverage), I grabbed my calculator, added up the cost of my previous year's doctors visits, compared the premiums and coverage of half a dozen individual and group plans, cross-referenced them with my estimated annual medical costs (that is, the ones I could predict), and checked to see which health plans my doctors participated in. Total pain in the ass. And not unlike trying to guess the number of jelly beans in a ten-gallon jar.

This year, I find myself shopping for a new health plan once again, as my monthly premiums recently spiked by 30 percent. Only this time, I plan to use an insurance agent a freelance pal recommended. (If you can't get a recommendation, at least contact an agent who's listed on NAHU.org.) Not only can an agent help you get the most bang for your insurance buck, they don't cost you a dime—the insurance companies pay their commissions.

Whatever you do, don't let your coverage lapse. If it does, due to some less-than-compassionate state laws, a future insurer could pull that "Sorry, no preexisting condition coverage for you!" crap that no patient wants to hear.

Insure Your Business's Ass

Every once in a while, I'll see someone make the wild claim in an online forum that freelancers who have a business license or have christened their business with a name other than their own are impervious from any legal war waged against them. But nothing could be further from the truth.

As we talked about in Chapter 4, incorporating your business or forming a limited liability company can help put a layer of protection between your personal assets (house, savings) and your professional life if you rack up business debt or find yourself on the losing end of a legal squabble with a client. But regardless of whether you form a corporation or LLC (or choose to remain a sole proprietor), if you feel at all legally vulnerable, you should look into professional liability insurance.

A professional liability policy can help protect a writer against a libel suit or a physical therapist against claims arising if a client takes a nasty spill in her office. Many indie professionals providing high stakes services (like financial counseling, web programming, and legal proofreading) also carry an errors & omissions (E&O) policy to help protect them in the event they screw up royally—say, if a web developer makes a critical mistake that leads to her client's e-commerce site being hacked (and a subsequent public relations fiasco). While a liability policy for $1 million (often the recommended bare minimum) can cost hundreds of dollars a year or more, if you're in a sue-happy industry, it could be the best investment you'll ever make.

If you're new to freelancing, a professional liability policy might sound like total overkill. (I certainly managed to avoid buying one for more than a decade.) But once you start meeting with clients at your office, farming out work to other freelancers, or working with big-fish clients like regional governments and Fortune 500 companies (some of whom will require you to carry liability insurance), business coverage becomes harder to avoid. Your best bet is to talk to a legal adviser (for recommendations, see pages 126–127) and some seasoned freelancers in your industry to find out what, if any, type of policy is standard for the work you do. Better to get the necessary policies in place—and boost your freelance rates to cover the cost—before you start negotiating contracts with *Fast Company*'s cover story du jour.

One more word to the wise: Being the proud owner of a pile of pricey computer and home office equipment also makes you a good candidate for business owner's insurance. Your homeowner's or renter's insurance won't adequately cover your business loot in the event of loss or damage. As always, tap your fellow freelancers for recommendations for commercial insurance agents, and make sure any agents you talk to understand that you're a business of one (as opposed to a fifty-employee firm with two hundred clients) so they price your policy accordingly.

When the 9-to-5 Devil Comes Calling

I thought of calling this section "Screw the Freelance Life" because frankly, all freelancers have weeks from hell when we fantasize about throwing in the towel. "If I had a day job, I wouldn't have to deal with these jokers and their ridiculous check-in-the-mail story," we tell ourselves. "If I had a day job, I could call in sick instead of working through a bad flu to make this deadline. If I had a day job, I wouldn't have to shell out thousands a year in health insurance. . . ."

And if, during a really bad week when every client is working your every last nerve, someone offers you $85,000 a year to do what you do as a freelancer, only on staff, with full benefits, a swanky office, some telecommuting privileges, and all the free office supplies you could want, you might find yourself sorely tempted. Especially if you just lost a big client, your last project nearly sent you to the ER, and you have $7,000 in credit card debt that you haven't been able to pay off since you don't know when.

I wouldn't blame you. I've been there many times, teetering on the edge, wondering if I should just jump. A couple times I even made it all the way to the job interview. And that yearlong full-time permalance gig I mentioned earlier? The only thing that made it not a regular day job was that it had an end date. It also made me crazy-miserable, just as I suspected it would, but it helped me pay off my debts in record time, which was priority number one for me that year.

So if the 9-to-5 (or 7-to-7) world makes you an offer you're not sure you can refuse, treat the decision just as you would a freelance job prospect:

- Get all the information you can about the position, company, your prospective teammates, the schedule, the perks, and anything else you can think of.

- Revisit the mini business plan you made in Chapter 1 to remind yourself of your freelance goals for the year.

- Be real about why you're considering the gig: Wanting to boost your skill set or needing the better health insurance plan because your kid is chronically sick is one thing. Being dazzled by the fancy title or corner office despite the job description boring you to tears isn't quite so compelling an argument.

- Make a pros-and-cons list for staying freelance, and one for taking the day job. Do you have a winner? If not, pretend you've decided to accept the gig. Is your gut screaming "No, no, for the love of God, N-frigging-O!"? If so, heed it.

- If your prevailing thought is "This job would be great if only I could telecommute a couple days a week, do it part-time, or do it on a temporary contract basis," negotiate for what you want. You already have a freelance business, so it's not like you have anything to lose.

Know this: Taking a temporary trip back to the cube doesn't mean you're a freelance failure. Instead, it can mean you're taking care of yourself. With any luck, you'll come away with a portfolio's worth of samples, a few dozen new contacts, some spiffy new skills, a nice cushion in your bank account, and a paid vacation or two. At the very least, you'll remember why you love freelancing so much.

Chapter 16

Pay the Piper

How to not piss off the IRS

"Oh, get bent, taxman!"

—Maggie Gyllenhaal in *Stranger Than Fiction*, 2006

I f you've never filed taxes as a freelancer before, it can be almost as spooky as watching *The Shining* alone in an empty house at 2:00 in the morning. But unless you want to follow in the footsteps of Leona "We Don't Pay Taxes" Helmsley (read: take an extended trip to the pokey), I suggest you listen up.

I won't lie to you: Paying your taxes as a self-employed person is a pain in the ass. As I said earlier in the book, we freelancers pay our taxes directly to the feds in estimated quarterly tax installments through-out the year; our clients don't take taxes out of our checks the way a 9-to-5 employer would. There's also a lovely little thing known as the self-employment tax we get to contend with, which basically means we pay both the employer and employee portion of our social security bill, amounting to about 15 percent of our annual freelance income.

As I mentioned in Chapter 4, I recommend hiring an accountant or CPA right away. Not only are they experts in deciphering hundreds of tax forms, it's their job to keep up on the ever-changing permutations of tax law. Yet many new freelancers try to cut costs by paying "a friend who's good at math" $100 to do their taxes. Unfortunately if that friend doesn't know diddly about freelance tax law, you could wind up being slapped with interest for underpaying Uncle Sam, as has happened to a couple of newbie freelancers I know—meaning you'll just wind up paying an accountant a few hundred bucks to help clean up the mess anyway. Besides, the annual fee you pay your tax preparer is an expense you can write off.

In Chapter 4, I also recommended hiring a tax professional who's experienced at working with freelancers, artists, or self-employed folks in your line of work. You don't want a tax preparer who only works with fifty-employee firms. You want someone who knows how to help an independent professional like you play by the rules and save as much as you can on your tax bill. For recommendations, one email to your favorite discussion list or post to your preferred web community usually does the trick.

For simplicity's sake, I'm going to assume in this chapter that you're running a sole proprietorship (an unincorporated business of one) as opposed to a partnership, corporation, LLC, or any other business entity. If you're not a sole proprietor, some of the advice in this chapter may not directly apply to you—except for my insistence that you hire a tax adviser immediately if you have not already done so.

Show Uncle Sam the Money

I'm no tax or financial professional myself, but I'm happy to give you the basics of what I've learned from my umpteen years of paying the IRS as a self-employed writer. Rule number one: Sock away a percentage of every dollar you earn until your estimated quarterly payments come due to the IRS on April 15, June 15, September 15, and January 15. Take it from someone who learned the hard way: Don't spend this money. Just pretend it isn't yours (because technically, it isn't) and put it in an interest-earning savings account until it's time to fork it over.

While the IRS doesn't require sole proprietors to open a business bank account, stashing your tax dollars in a savings account other than the one you keep for personal use is a good idea. You'll be less tempted to touch it. Since many banks charge higher fees for business accounts, just open a new personal account. If you're good about paying off your credit card bills each month, I suggest getting a separate credit card you can use for all your business expenses, too. It'll help you keep cleaner records. Who knows? You may even earn enough points for a new coffee maker.

How much should you save? "Plan on a minimum of 25 to 30 cents on every dollar you bring in going to taxes," says tax professional Elizabeth Mance of Accountability Services, a small business tax firm based in Seattle. I save about a third of my income for taxes, but depending on how much you earn, any other sources of income you have, and a whole host of things I can't even begin to imagine, this number will vary from freelancer to freelancer. (See why you need a tax professional?)

A lot of rookie and veteran freelancers ask me why they need to pay their quarterly taxes. "Why can't I just invest that money and pay the government one lump sum come April 15?" they want to know. But paying Uncle Sam as you go is a fact of freelance life, just like staff meetings were part of your day job in your former 9-to-5 life. If you don't pay quarterly, the IRS is all too happy to charge you interest on April 15, and their rates are not cheap. Keep in mind that you're just paying an *estimate* of the taxes you owe each quarter, so if you're a few hundred bucks shy of the total owed on April 15, the interest will be tiny.

Depending on your local laws and how much income you make, you may also owe city and state taxes, sometimes called a business license tax, at the end of the calendar year (these aren't paid quarterly). If you register for a city and/or state business license (covered in Chapter 4), the city and state government agencies you register with can fill you in on the details, as can your accountant. City and state tax forms can be much easier to navigate than their IRS counterparts. I've gotten away with having my accountant walk me through them the first year, then filling them out myself after that.

W-9, 1099, 1040-ES, OMG!

A few IRS tax forms are crucial for making your quarterly tax payments:

W-9. In order to pay you, your clients need you to fill out this short form, which, among other things, asks you to list a taxpayer identification number. While your social security number will suffice, many freelancers like to use an employer identification number (EIN) instead for extra protection against identity theft. You can apply for an EIN online at IRS.gov. It's free and it only takes a couple minutes.

1099-MISC. Each client who pays you at least $600 in the calendar year is required to send you this simple form by February of the following year. All you need to do with this form is check that it matches your income records (clients do make mistakes) and give it to your accountant at tax time. If a client who pays you more than $600 during the year fails to send you a 1099 (their bad in the IRS's eyes, not yours), you still have to pay taxes on that income. Ditto for any income you earn from a particular client totaling less than $600 that year.

1040-ES. Mail in your quarterly tax payments with the vouchers provided on this form (a.k.a. Estimated Tax for Individuals). Or follow the form's directions for electronic payment. If you know your way around federal forms, the 1040-ES can help you calculate your quarterly tax payments; otherwise, it's about as clear as mud.

You can download any of these forms, plus countless others, from IRS .gov, which is surprisingly informative *and* easy to navigate. Don't worry if you can't make heads or tails of a particular form or law though. Any tax preparer worth her salt should be happy to explain the essentials to you.

Anal Like Me: Why You Need to Track Your Business Expenses and How to Painlessly Do So

Obviously, writing off business expenses can help lower your tax bill, but before we get into what you can deduct, let's talk about how to track your expenses.

Basically, you need a system. You need to save every receipt for every business-related expense you plan to deduct on your tax return. (If you have the misfortune of getting audited, the IRS will want to see those receipts.) Bank and credit card statements won't cut it; you need hard copies of receipts. If you buy something on the web, print out the receipt. If you take a client to dinner, note on the receipt who you met and what you discussed so you're not left wondering what the receipt is for later. If you drive a lot for your work (real estate agent, traveling masseuse, and so on), keep a notebook in your car for tracking your business mileage.

Get yourself a fat accordion folder and file your receipts by category—office expenses, dinners with clients, trade magazine subscriptions, and so on. Come tax time, you'll need to give those expense category totals to your accountant. (More on expense categories in the next section.) While many tax professionals recommend entering all your receipts into an accounting program like Tax MiniMiser (www.tax minimiser.com), Quicken, or QuickBooks, some freelancers—ahem!—still rely on the do-it-yourself Excel spreadsheet method. If you do want to try an automated program, though, QuickBooks Simple Start is free (http://quickbooks.intuit.com).

Entering your receipts as you go—say, weekly or monthly—can make this chore much easier. Don't throw everything in one shoebox and wait until April 1 to sort it all out like I did for many years. You'll curse yourself for doing so. Not only can those little white and yellow slips fade and get lost, they have the uncanny ability to make one lose her mind when stored in vast quantities.

How long do you need to keep this mountain of paperwork for? Experts say to hold on to your tax returns, expense reports, and expense receipts for seven years, then shred like the dickens.

Can I Write It Off?

A good accountant or CPA can help lower your taxes by ensuring you claim all the legitimate deductions you're allowed. She'll also stop you from making boneheaded expense claims that could get you into trouble with Big Brother (for example, multiplying the 250 hours you spent blogging last year by your hourly rate and trying to write off the total as "advertising").

To see all the business expenses you can claim on your federal tax return, go to IRS.gov and search on the form called Schedule C (a.k.a. Profit or Loss from Business). See Part II on the form, which lists twenty different types of expenses. Again, this is only for sole proprietorships.

So which business expenses are deductible? Those most applicable to new freelancers include:

- Advertising (business cards and online ads included)
- Business insurance (but not health insurance; see next page)
- Business and professional licenses
- Business phone and Internet access
- Client gifts (you can only deduct $25 per client a year)
- Industry-related books, classes, and events
- Interest on business credit cards and loans (must be used solely for business)
- Memberships to professional associations

- Office space rental, utilities, and expenses
- Office supplies and equipment, as well as any necessary repairs
- PO box, postage, shipping costs, and photocopies
- Professional services (lawyer, accountant, web designer)
- Public transportation (to business-related meetings and events)
- Subscriptions to industry publications and services

A few other write-offs warrant a bit more explanation:

CAR AND TRUCK EXPENSES. There are two ways to write off the business use of your automobile. You can claim the cost of repairs, gas, insurance, registration, and the like—what the IRS calls the "actual expense" method. Or if you've carefully documented your business mileage (here's where that notebook in the car comes in handy), you can use what Uncle Sam calls the "standard mileage rate" method, meaning you deduct a fixed amount per mile (58.5 cents as of July 1, 2008; the IRS raises this periodically). Use whichever method yields you the biggest deduction, but know that you can't use the actual method one year and then switch to the standard method the next. So if you want to use the standard method, do it from the start. Either way, you can claim parking and tolls as an expense.

HEALTH INSURANCE. While we sole proprietors can't deduct our health insurance premiums on our Schedule C form, where it would save us the most money as self-employed professionals, we can deduct this cost on the main part of our Form 1040 (a.k.a., Individual Income Tax Return). Your tax preparer knows all about this; all you need to do is provide her with the amount you spend on health insurance premiums each year.

TRAVEL, MEALS, AND ENTERTAINMENT. If you take a potential new client to dinner, you can write off 50 percent of the restaurant bill. Don't go crazy though. A bunch of $500 dinner bills may cause the IRS to raise an eyebrow. Business trips and conventions are deductible, too. For a bigger tax savings, you can schedule a couple of business meetings or presentations during a personal vacation and write off part of the trip. (Your accountant can help you determine how much.)

HOME OFFICE. If you work from home, you can deduct your office space if you use the space strictly for business (it shouldn't double as a guest or storage room), you use it regularly (not just a couple times a month), and it's contained in one nice, neat area (as opposed to three different corners of your house). Basically, you measure your office and deduct whatever percentage of your home it amounts to on your tax return (mine's 30 percent). You can also deduct this same percentage of your home utility bills.

Note that if you've been in business three years without making a profit but continue to deduct your professional expenses (photography equipment, Internet access, computer software), you're asking for trouble—in other words, an audit. The IRS will consider you a hobbyist rather than a business owner, meaning your deductions won't be justified (meaning you'll probably owe back taxes, plus interest).

You may have heard it said that you should incorporate your business to reduce the amount of taxes you owe. But when you're just starting to freelance this isn't such a hot idea. Reason being, until you're really raking it in (something closer to six figures) you probably won't see the financial payoff. "You might be able to save yourself a few bucks in taxes, but those tax savings dollars will quickly get eaten up with incorporation costs, accounting costs, and administration costs," says Elizabeth, the tax adviser.

I'd understand if your eyes are starting to glaze over. But really, this isn't neuroscience; it's record keeping, filing, and data entry. You'll give your tax preparer all your 1099 forms, details about any other income you earned during the year, the expense report you created in your accounting or spreadsheet program (you keep the receipts), details on the size of your home office and the utilities you need to deduct, and if you moved since filing your last tax return, your current address.

A good tax preparer will walk you through the process, let you know if she needs any additional information from you, and make the process as painless as possible. When she's done working her accounting magic, she'll mail you your tax return to sign. Then you'll mail it in (along with any money you owe) to Uncle Sam, curse the feds for wasting your hard-earned tax dollars on programs you don't support, stick a copy of the completed return in your filing cabinet, and wash your hands of the whole matter until the following year.

Chapter 17

Fun with Time Management
Stop wasting time, start asking for help, and get a life outside work

"Lunch is for wimps."

—Michael Douglas in *Wall Street*, 1987

Working for yourself means being one part task mistress, one part zen mistress. Now that nothing's stopping you from crawling back into bed for the next six hours or watching court TV from dawn till dusk, you need structure, routine. With no boss cruising the halls, you need to prioritize your brains out and light a blowtorch under your own arse. At the same time, you need to be flexible enough to accommodate the star client who calls with a quick question about the rough draft or design specs you turned in the week before. And you need the calm, laserlike focus of the Super Nanny so you can return to the task at hand as soon as you're done tending to the interruption.

What you don't need, however, is some elaborate "productivity system" or a spreadsheet that maps—to the minute—when you plan to eat, piss, pet your dog, call client A, email client B, and sweet-talk client C each day. When it comes to time management, less is more. So in the interest of expediency, let's dive right in.

Yes, Mistress! (How to Crack Your Own Whip)

Your first order of business, if you haven't done so already, should be to set some office hours for yourself. If you have kids, your hours will likely be "whenever little Lyle is at school or daycare." If you don't, four hours of work can easily expand to fill the sixteen hours of unclaimed time you have each weekday if you're not careful.

To set your hours, figure out when you're sharpest and most productive (for me, it's 8:00 or 9:00 AM till 4:00 or 5:00 PM), then factor in when your clients are open for business. Ideally you want your customers to be able to reach you during at least 50 or 60 percent of their workday, even if it means you have to get up a tad earlier than normal because your clients are in an earlier time zone. Then let your customers know what your hours are. The sooner you start training them, the less likely they'll be to call you during *Project Runway*.

But being a beacon of freelance efficiency doesn't begin and end with setting office hours. Some additional suggestions:

DON'T DO LUNCH. To me, lunch dates with freelance friends are for days off, not workdays. Don't kid yourself into thinking that lunch takes just an hour—with travel time, it's two or three hours, minimum. Factor in someone showing up half an hour late, taking a bunch of client calls during the meal, or talking you into three rounds of margaritas, and you've blown the entire afternoon. You're better off meeting for dinner or happy hour after you've finished your work.

HAVE A WEEKLY CATCH-UP DAY. Rather than trying to stay on top of all your admin work throughout the week, save the less-pressing stuff (invoicing, filing, low-priority emailing) for one day or afternoon each week. Web designer Colleen Lynn often uses Fridays as her "down day" to catch up on administrata and her own design projects. Besides having those "low-stress" caps on the week to look forward to, she stays focused on the deadlines at hand Mondays through Thursdays (meeting them sooner than if she'd flitted from design project to marketing letter to invoice spreadsheet and back again each day).

LET TECHNOLOGY LIBERATE YOU. I know I told you in Chapter 4 not to go nuts on the office accoutrements, but if a $250 gadget allows you to work faster or smarter, by all means, go for it. Case in point: The twenty-one-inch flat-screen computer monitor I bought in 2007 ($300) was one of the best business purchases I've ever made. It's hard to believe now that I went so long without seeing the article I'm writing and my interview notes side by side. Ditto for the digital tape recorder I bought in 2006 ($80). Never again will I think up and promptly forget a so-called "brilliant idea" while walking my dog. And although I have yet to break down and get a CrackBerry, I know loads of freelancers who swear by theirs. Now that there's no chance they'll miss an important email from a steady or prospective client, many of these freelancers actually leave the house. Multiple times a day!

TRACK YOUR TIME OBSESSIVELY. Obviously you want to make as much money for as few hours worked as possible, and you want to estimate how long new projects will take as accurately as you can. A web-based time-tracking tool like MyHours.com (free, as I write this) can help, especially if you're a chronic underestimator (one of my big shortcomings). Seeing that a $500 project has taken you 50 hours to complete can help you determine whether you need to work faster or raise your rates for a similar project next time. (Hint: You could probably stand to do both.)

KNOW WHEN TO SAY "WHEN." We talked about saying no to projects that fall outside your area of expertise or have too many red flags earlier in the book. But what about saying no to something that sounds positively thrilling when you're positively booked? Lord knows I'm a long-time sufferer of "biting off more than I can chew" syndrome. But here's another mistake of mine you can learn from: A great gig won't be great for your career if you can't do it justice—or worse, if you royally screw it up—because you're already drowning in deadlines. Remember, your name's going on that half-coherent comic strip you drew or software code you wrote at 4:00 AM on zero sleep. If you can't humanly swing it, tell the client how eager you are to work for them and let them know how soon you'll be available for future projects.

Call the Babysitter

If your waist-high family members aren't in school yet, don't kid yourself that you'll be able to work from home for a concentrated period of time unless another adult is there to help (be they a sitter, nanny, friend, relative, or domestic partner). All the freelance moms I've talked to work around their kids' sleep or childcare schedules. But they do make it work. Seattle-based food and lifestyle writer Sarah Jio, a self-described "hands-on mom," is a shining example. She does most of her work on the magazine articles she writes while her baby naps, after he goes to sleep at night, and in the wee morning hours before he wakes (conveniently, her East Coast sources are up by 6:00 AM her time).

"There have also been times when an editor has needed something ASAP, and I've had to call my husband home from work to watch the baby while I did an interview or worked on an article's revisions," Sarah adds. "He's not always able to drop everything and come help me, but when he's had a free lunch hour, he has been happy to lend a hand."

Now if that's not supporting the arts, I don't know what is.

Stupid Zen Tricks (Mind Games for Beginners)

"I've always resisted the idea that being able to freelance is somehow noble or requires more discipline or skill," says writer Lynn Harris. "People who work in an office have the same video games on the computer."

Still, those cube dwellers have the fear of being caught playing solitaire by their managers to keep them in line. But with the help of a few mind games, you too can force yourself to stay on track throughout the workday. Start your day off with a ritual—a brisk walk, a strong cappuccino, a Motown dance number. Shower and dress if that makes you feel more productive. Don't if gussying up makes you feel like hitting the town instead of working. (My happy medium: changing from my "sleeping" pajamas to my "working" pajamas.) If you need a creative shot in the arm, switch up your routine: Adopt a new morning ritual. Move your computer to another room. Do an errand mid-morning if you don't normally leave the house till 5:00. Get a theme song.

A few more things I've learned over the years about playing tricks on yourself:

LIMIT YOUR DAILY TO-DO LIST TO FIVE ITEMS. Don't think for a minute that you can work on seventeen projects in a day. Nothing stresses me out like starting the day with a to-do list jam-packed with more than a dozen starred, highlighted, exclamation-pointed items. Instead, give yourself one or two big tasks to tackle first (draft an article, redesign a web page) when you're most fresh and a handful of little ones to cap off the day with (calls to return, research to do, samples to send to the dreamy would-be client who contacted you the day before). For additional peace of mind, make tomorrow's to-do list before you call it a day.

HAVE SOMEWHERE TO BE "AFTER WORK." You may have heard it said that the freelancer with a full day's worth of work is far more productive than the freelancer with just a couple hours of to-do's on her plate. It's true that nothing gets you cranking like knowing that another task needs finishing before the day's out. On the flip side, nothing breeds "it took me twelve hours to do a three-hour gig" syndrome like having too little to do. My suggestion to those still building up their workload: Make plans to meet a friend, run an errand, or get some exercise at the end of the day so your afternoon has a finite cap on it.

PRETEND IT'S SATURDAY. I used to love working on Saturdays because my phone wouldn't ring and my inbox wouldn't ding. For me, the day is pretty much distraction-free. Then it dawned on me: I was working *on Saturdays*. So rather than eliminate distractions by working through the weekend, I do my best to eliminate them Monday through Friday and save Saturdays at "the office" for emergencies.

When I'm on deadline, I can't have the TV on, my best friend from high school IMing me, or my email chiming every five minutes. Even my cell phone vibrating stresses me out. Same goes for the dog pacing around my office. So I close and unplug everything I can, and I kick everyone out. I encourage anyone who might need me to email rather than call. I'll still check the ole inbox several times during the day (or leave email on but set to mute if I'm expecting an important message), but unless it's pressing, don't expect to hear back from me until the end of the day.

As for the Internet, that's a toughie. If you're a wordsmith, designer, or developer, you're probably accustomed to researching as you work— the correct spelling of "mnemonic," the HTML code for magenta. I'm sure you've noticed, though, that when you hit Pause on your concentration to Google something, it takes a few seconds to figure out what the heck you were just doing and ease back into the project on your plate (if you succumbed to the siren call of YouTube along the way, make that a few minutes—or hours). So whenever possible, I try to plow ahead with my assignment sans Internet, stick an "X" where any missing details need to go, and fact-check later. In the words of *Guardian* writer Tim Dowling, working with your web browser open is "really a question of whether the time saved outweighs the time you spend watching a YouTube video of a monkey drinking its own pee."

FORGET EXTRA CREDIT. I understand wanting to knock every job you do for a client out of the ballpark. But interviewing seven sources instead of the one the client requested or creating five different versions of the home page for them to choose from instead of the two they asked for is way over the top. Besides driving your price-per-hour down with all that additional work, your excesses will likely go unnoticed by the client (unless you actually turn in all your extra work, giving your client more content to wade through, which they're not likely to appreciate).

Now before you tell me you're no extra credit junkie, track a handful of your projects with MyHours.com or your tool of choice. Break down your work on each project by steps (research, execution, revisions, and so on). If you're doing fifteen hours of research for a $500 project that takes five hours to draft, draw, or otherwise produce, you're probably an extra credit junkie. (Take it from one in recovery.) As they say in Hollywood, stop auditioning—you already got the job.

SLEEP YOUR WAY TO THE TOP. I'm not much for caffeine these days, which means if I don't get seven or eight hours of sleep the night before, I'm useless by 1:00 PM. Fortunately, I'm a big fan of the abbreviated siesta. Give me a good twenty- or thirty-minute snooze at lunch and I can crank out copy for the rest of the day, no problem. I realize you may not have the luxury of napping through lunch (on many days I don't either). But if you hit that exhaustion wall and you do have the time, try sleeping it off for a few minutes. It's much cheaper than a latte.

How to Lose Friends and Alienate Family

It's a scientific fact that friends and family will have a hard time understanding that even though you're home, you're not available to pick up their dry cleaning, have them over for lunch, chat on the phone for forty-five minutes while they're stuck in traffic, or otherwise serve, amuse, or host them during the workday.

"You have to just get comfortable with saying 'No, I can't go grocery shopping today. Just because I'm in my pajamas doesn't mean that I'm not working,'" writer Meghan Daum says. "I don't think people have mal intent. I just think there's a psychic connection that needs to be made where you realize the person is working."

Because this psychic connection can take years to make (even today, people ask me if they can "stop by for an hour" in the middle of my workday), strict monitoring of your phone calls is imperative. Never answer without checking caller ID. Even better, get a separate business line and don't give the number to anyone who isn't paying you.

⇨

⇨

It's also a scientific fact that some acquaintances will have a hard time accepting that you need to bail on even the most tentative of dinner plans if the dream project you've been hoping for unexpectedly lands in your lap and you need to work overtime to squeeze it in. Rather than nurse my rep as "she who always cancels" (caught again!), I'm working a new strategy: committing to only the most important of social outings (birthdays, bat mitzvahs, book launch parties). Your 9-to-5 friends with kids, grad school papers due, and big presentations at the office to prep for aren't available every time someone decides to have a poker party on a Monday night, so why should you be? If your wage-earning friends can't hang with your freelance life ("What do you *mean* you don't know if you'll be free seven Thursday nights from now?"), it might be time for a few new friends.

Since you have so much in common with other freelancers, you'll likely find yourself cultivating more and more of those friendships anyway. Take photographer Dani Weiss, who predominantly shoots weddings and other weekend events. "People are really only available for dinner during the week, but I like to go for a daytime walk with my friends," she says. "So I tend to hang out with a lot of other wedding photographers. Most of my friends don't have day jobs." Not only will your fellow indie professionals understand if you have to play Friday night's happy hour invite by ear or pass on Saturday afternoon's barbeque, chances are they've got a killer assignment they're crunching on too.

Get Some Professional Help

If you find yourself spending much of the day trying to keep up with all the administrative tasks your hopping freelance business generates before you can even turn to the work your clients are hiring you to do, it's time to hire another set of hands. Start with an intern (easy to find through your local university) or a virtual assistant (suggestions for where to look in the Resource Guide).

Yes, you'll initially have to invest some time explaining what you'd like done, and yes, your right-hand gal (or guy) might not perform certain tasks the same way you would have. But if the result is the same and you're freeing up valuable time you need to get your billable work done, does it really matter?

Though I've had a couple of assistants and interns over the past few years and I've subcontracted a bit of work to other freelancers in the past decade, I'm admittedly a novice at this crazy little thing called delegating. So I asked virtual assistant Erin Blaskie of Business Services, ETC, who manages a team of ten VAs, for her best tips on handing off work to others. Her golden rules for delegating:

- Hand off any tasks you hate to do.
- Hand off any tasks you do repeatedly each day or week.
- Hand off the tasks that will be easiest to teach someone else to do.
- Think about delegating an entire "department" of your business, such as accounts receivable or market research.
- Hand off tasks you can't bill your clients for, and focus on doing the billable work yourself.

Before you start handing off projects, track all the time you spend at work for a week or two in a tool like MyHours.com, from billable hours to client correspondence to Google searches. Now revisit the previous list. See any dreaded or nonbillable tasks tying up a pretty large chunk of your workweek? Then delegate away!

"Outsourcing should not cost you money," Erin says. "It should make you money." Think about it: If paying an assistant $25 to $50 an hour frees up five hours of your week for billable work and you're charging your clients $100 an hour, you stand to make $250 to $375 more a week.

Photographer Anne Ruthmann is the perfect case study. "Processing digital images bores me to death," she says. "I'd literally fall asleep at my computer." More important, processing her photos was incredibly time consuming, accounting for at least 50 percent of her schedule. Once she factored in the other administrata of her business, she was only shooting pictures 25 percent of the week. By farming out her processing, though, she's now able to do far more shoots, which means she brings home more bacon.

Still, as a lone freelancer, you can only make as much as your billable rate multiplied by the hours you're able to work each year, unless you farm out some of the billable work to other freelancers and take a cut off the top. If you're getting offered more billable work than you can handle, subcontracting like this can be a great way to keep your client, keep your workload manageable, and harvest some extra green. Note that you'll need your client's approval before you can outsource part of a job they're hiring you to do—they may not be amenable to this setup (it likely will say so right in your contract).

Before you farm out work to other freelancers, you'll need to draw up a contract outlining the terms of your working relationship with them. Now that you've stepped into the role of "client," you'll want to ensure that your subcontractors don't poach your own clients, and you'll want to get it in writing. Here's one instance when I wouldn't skimp on hiring a legal adviser to make sure your contracts are up to snuff. For help finding legal aid, see the sidebar in Chapter 12. You'll also need to pay your subcontractors directly and send them a 1099 form in January if you paid them more than $600 the previous calendar year. Definitely discuss this with your accountant to make sure you engage in the appropriate amount of ass-covering.

Subcontracting often involves finding, screening, hiring, training, and managing the freelancers you outsource to. Since the quality of your subcontractors' work is on your head, you'll want to check it—at least until you get to know and trust them—before sending it off to your client. This is in fact what the client is paying you for: overseeing a team of independent professionals so they don't have to.

Not surprisingly, you'll want to boost your rates to account for the management and recruiting aspect of the work you're now doing for such clients. Freelancers who hire subcontractors take a cut ranging anywhere from 15 to 35 percent off the top of what they pay their subs, sometimes even more. The price you're able to charge your client for the job and the rate you need to pay a qualified subcontractor will largely dictate the amount of your cut. Just be sure you're adequately compensated for your own time and expenses.

Vacation, All I Ever Wanted

"I learned fairly early on that you just have to schedule vacations ahead of time, block out the time on the calendar, don't accept any work then, and go," says editor Sherri Schultz. "If you wait for a time when you 'don't have any work,' it never comes."

Your best bet is to plan any and all big trips at the start of the year and, if possible, buy your plane tickets or book your lodging right away so you can't back out later if work gets too hairy. I aspire to be like Sarah Haynes, owner of The Spitfire Agency, a Northern California–based fundraising event firm. Each fall, she sets aside a few weeks to cruise around the country in her restored 1967 Airstream Caravel. "I work through Christmas and I work through every other holiday because I love taking extended periods of time off," she says. "I plan it really well." (Indeed!)

Some additional tips for vacationing freelancers:

CLUE IN YOUR CLIENTS. Give any customers you're currently working with plenty of warning about your out-of-office dates and make sure you tie up any loose ends on your projects before you go. Remember, clients don't like surprises.

UNPLUG. Seriously. Be reachable by mobile device in case of emergencies if you must, but don't bring projects to work on. Why spend two days of your trip stuck in an Internet café if you don't have to? I'd rather have a more distinct line between work and play, even if it means taking a five-day trip instead of a seven-day one.

CUSHION THE BLOW. Nothing is worse than racing to make a deadline four hours before your plane leaves. (Yeah, been there too.) Instead, give yourself a two-day cushion before big trips: one day for any last-minute work issues that crop up (quick client questions, lost invoices, and the like), the other for all the pretravel personal errands you need to run.

Get over the notion that if you leave town, the world will slip off its axis and your freelance life will come to a screeching, permanent halt. None of this will happen. I promise.

Step Away from the Computer!

Let's be honest: A lot of new freelancers work more than forty hours a week. Hell, a lot of seasoned ones do (again, guilty as charged). Between all the marketing and making ends meet and the heroic efforts to impress hotshot new clients you've been courting, overtime happens.

Many of us are so jazzed by the work we do that we don't mind a little overwork now and then. But it's when those sixty-hour weeks become the norm that you might want to take a step back and reassess— or at the very least, shut down your computer, get the heck out of the house, and think about something other than working for the next few hours. There's a fine line between being a superstar and being the freelancer who misses her ailing pop's birthday party because she's stuck at work à la *Ugly Betty*.

Make it your mission in life to avoid Monday deadlines like the plague. Even if your client gives you no say in the due date, consider your deadline the Friday before. Take it from someone who'd like her last umpteen weekends back: Saturdays and Sundays were made for slacking.

"The flip side of success is that you never get away from work," says Wendy Merrill, owner of WAM Marketing Group. "It took me a while to be disciplined enough to be home and be working. And now it's like, How do I take time out for lunch and not be sitting at my computer all day or go for a walk and go to yoga?"

In the interest of gaining some semblance of balance, I suggest building a bit of structured downtime into your workweek. (Walking from your computer to your television doesn't count.) My dog coaxes me out of the house and into the neighborhood park many a morning and late afternoon. Wendy volunteers with homeless kids every Friday from 2:00 to 5:00 PM. And personal trainer Alisa Geller, a woman after my own heart, does not schedule any clients between noon and 3:00 PM. Instead, she heads home, fixes herself lunch, walks her dog, and takes a nice fat nap. Every Monday through Friday.

Don't overlook the value in getting far, far away from your work as often as possible and taking the time to recharge. A fried freelancer is of no use to herself and her clients. If you're having trouble concentrating and pulling your weight on even the most routine of projects, what are you going to do when the stuff really hits the fan?

Chapter 18

Your Master Plan for World Domination

Raise your rates, promote yourself like crazy, and do the work you really want to do

"I'm famous. That's my job."

—Jerry Rubin

"Where do you see yourself in five years?" will probably go down in history as the dumbest job interview question ever invented by middle management. But in the context of developing your freelance career, there's some real merit to looking down the road three, five, even ten years. That's why I asked you to write down your goals in Chapter 1 and your Top Ten client list in Chapter 8. Because if you don't keep your eyes on the road ahead, it's all too easy to lose your bearings and wind up miles from where you thought you were headed.

As I said at the start of the book, there's no one formula for freelance success. For some, the dream is to substitute as much of the bread-and-butter work with the paid creative work they really want to do—be that illustrating books, performing in nightclubs, or selling screenplays. For others, it's to trade in their hired-gun hat for that of management and grow their business of one into a twelve-person creative agency. Still others aim to make such an impressive chunk of change that they can afford to take four days off every week, donate 15 percent of their profits to charity, or globetrot two or three months a year.

No matter what your destination, something tells me you'll be able to relate to illustrator Molly Crabapple, who says, "I have had a master plan since I was seven." In fact, I have yet to meet a freelancer who isn't looking to boost her income, spread the word about her talents from Kansas to Cannes, and do as many "pinch me—I'm dreaming!" projects as soon as humanly possible. So in the name of making the world drop to its collective knees and offer you the keys to the freelance kingdom, let's talk about how you can do all three.

Give Yourself a Raise

I hate to break it to you, but in my umpteen years of freelancing, not once has a steady client said to me or any other freelancer I know, "You do such great work for us that we'd like to bump up your pay by 25 percent. Is that okay with you?" Unfortunately, it doesn't work this way. Instead, we indie professionals need to create our own pay raises. Besides helping us keep up with the cost of living, it's one of the best ways we have to measure how much we've grown as self-employed professionals.

Just as there's no one right way to build a freelance career, there's no one way to break the news to a longtime client that you're raising your rates. If you're a dog walker, cosmetologist, or business consultant with standard session or project rates and dozens of clients on your schedule each month, snail mailing a letter to your customers to tell them how much you love them and appreciate their business—and that due to increasing operating costs, you're raising your rates effective the first of [whatever month you've determined]—is the easiest and most considerate way to address this. (To me, email feels cheesy in this instance; plus, it's too easy for bulk emails to get lost or tossed without being read.)

Give your existing clients two or three months' notice so they're not blindsided by this change, but charge any new customers who walk through your door your new rate, effective immediately. There's no reason to tell them that you just raised your rates. You have nothing to gain by oversharing that nugget of information.

If, however, you only work for a handful of clients each month and your rates vary wildly depending on project scope and industry (for example, if half your clients are nonprofit arts organizations and half are Fortune 500 biotech firms), skip the letter in favor of a phone conversation. The next time the client offers you a project, explain how much you heart them and the work they feed you but that all your other clients are paying you at least [whatever rate you'd like them to come up to] and you need to start charging them that amount too. Be confident and concise, just as we discussed in Chapter 11; don't whine, beg, or mention your staggering student loans. Remember, you're a professional, not their Thursday night beer buddy.

Some clients will shoot you down; when asking for extra green, I've won some and I've lost some. But if a client's costing me potential income by refusing to pay me the rate I know I can make elsewhere, it won't be long before I trade up to a customer who can afford to pay me more. I may love the work and the PIE (exposure) the client offers, but usually I'll start cutting back on how many assignments I can take from them right away. And once I find a comparable company or media outlet to work for (usually within three to six months), I'm out of there, just like an employee who gets a better day-job offer.

Rekindling a relationship with a client you haven't worked for in six months or more makes a fantastic opportunity to increase your rates. Often a client who's been off your radar awhile will say, "Remind me of your rate again?" when you're discussing the terms of the project. But regardless of whether they do ask, if you haven't raised your rates with them in at least a year, you're in a great position to say "I'm now charging $80 an hour for this type of work." End of story. No need to do a song and dance about the rising price of gasoline or paperclips since you last spoke. This is just the rate you command now because you're that fabulous.

So how often should you bump up your rates as a rule, and by how much? Raise them by at least 5 percent a year or 10 percent every two years, says Mikelann Valterra, director of The Women's Earning Institute in Seattle, which has been advising self-employed women on how to earn their worth for almost a decade.

Don't worry about some clients dropping off your radar. "Not everyone should be able to afford you," Mikelann says. "If everyone can afford you, you're not charging enough money. You need to lose some clients off the bottom to make room for clients at the top."

That said, be careful not to ask for the sun, the moon, *and* the paid subscription to Starz. "If you're brand-new and you've got 50 percent of people walking away from you, that says that (a) your price is too high, or (b) you're not talking to the right people," Mikelann says. For freelancers who've been in business just a couple years, 20 percent price resistance is more like it.

If you own the copyrights to your creative work (as you should; see Chapter 12), you can reduce your hours worked and boost your income by reselling or repurposing your writing, illustrations, or photographs. We journalists will resell or cannibalize our stories whenever possible. Failing that, we'll sell two or more stories on the same topic to noncompeting markets to maximize our research. On the visual arts side, Molly Crabapple sells originals of the promotional posters, magazine covers, and other illustrations she's been commissioned to do right off her website. And artist Nikki McClure, who says she's all about "less images, more money," has recycled and retooled her popular image of a diver, called *Return* and first created for a 2000 calendar she self-published, seven times.

If you're thinking you couldn't possibly ask your clients for more money because you haven't been working solo five to ten years or you don't have twenty-five clients in your portfolio yet or you haven't taken that project management class you've been wanting to take, stop right there. The time to start keeping up with the cost of living is now, not three years from now. None of us will ever be 100 percent perfect, no matter how much experience we gain. So we might as well stop waiting for that mythical day when the heavens part and the freelance gods place a gold star on the lapels of our Adidas track suit and instead charge what we're worth today.

Bride of the Son of Shameless Self-Promotion on Steroids

When you're a rookie freelancer—and even when you're an old salt like me—you probably won't have much cash on hand to spend on marketing and advertising each year. You'll obviously want to build and maintain a website, as we discussed in Chapter 5. Likewise, it's worth spending a hundred dollars or so to join a professional association that goes out of its way to refer potential customers to its members (not to mention offers legal advice and a health plan).

You might also decide it's worth your while to attend a $300 to $500 industry conference if you stand to learn some valuable new skills or insider information, or if the event promises to be a feeding ground for dozens of potential clients. But I wouldn't encourage you to rush out and spend several hundred or several thousand dollars on web or print ads right away, at least not until you've exhausted all the other work-hunting tactics discussed in Part 2.

The good news, as you already saw, is that most freelancers become hot commodities simply by doing stellar work and racking up the referrals. That said, there is some variance from industry to industry; wedding photographers, marriage counselors, and dog walkers are more likely to advertise than, say, writers, cartoonists, and filmmakers. But whether you're a therapist whose client list is looking a little lean or a painter eager to propel herself into the spotlight, there are loads of ways for you to spread the word about your talents on the cheap. More often than not, all that's required is an investment of your time.

This section highlights some of my favorite ways to get your name out there, several of which can even earn you some cash in the process.

Because any time you invest in unpaid marketing efforts is time you can't devote to paid (billable) work, think long and hard before you rush into any self-promo tactics that require more than an hour of your time. Spend a few hours at the end of the year talking to other freelancers in your trade about which marketing tactics have paid off for them and which have bombed. Don't commit to anything unless you know why you're doing it and what you stand to gain from it. Then, at the start of the new year, decide where you'll invest your marketing efforts and commit these goals to paper, right in your Business Plan To Go for the year.

JOIN A PLANNING COMMITTEE. Donating your ideas, talents, and organizational skills to a high-visibility pro bono project (an AIDS walk, an arts conference) can pay off in contacts, client referrals, and that almighty PIE. When I moved to Seattle in the late nineties, I wanted to catapult myself into the center of the local writing and book publishing community, so I volunteered to work on a planning committee of Northwest Bookfest (sadly now defunct). Not only did the experience land me several clients, it yielded some freelance friends that I'll probably have for life.

PLAY EMCEE. In addition to helping plan a number of panels on writing at Northwest Bookfest, I offered to moderate a couple of them, which basically entailed greasing the conversation onstage and which put me in contact with some leading industry players in my region. And in the late-nineties dot-com heyday, I was paid to write a weekly column on freelance web writing opportunities by a well-known website about—you guessed it—web content (also now retired), which meant I had to find and interview countless hotshot new web companies, several of which became my clients in the process.

Anytime you have the chance to interview, moderate, host, or otherwise rub elbows with experts in your field on more of a peer level (as opposed to the gal who simply hands them a water bottle before their talk gets underway), you have the chance to make a lasting connection.

When you do meet these experts, play it cool. Ask them about themselves, their work, or their philosophies rather than bulldozing forward with "OMG, it's so totally unbelievable to meet you! Can I send you my demo/manuscript/portfolio so you can help me get an agent/a book deal/a job?" If you listen, you're bound to get some invaluable tips. If you're gracious, you may even get their card or an invitation to contact them with additional questions.

SHOWCASE YOUR TALENTS. In 1997, Nikki McClure created a 1998 wall calendar during the span of a month, ran off a few hundred copies at Kinko's, and wound up selling 300 copies between December 1997 and January 1998. "I don't have a portfolio—my calendar is that," Nikki says. "All these creative professionals are getting it as gifts, so I've been getting all these jobs from that." But her calendar is so much more than a calling card or portfolio. In 2008, her annual calendar sold 17,000 copies. On BuyOlympia.com, her calendar sells for $16.00. Even with her distributor taking a cut of the profits, this is one promo tool that pays for itself a bazillion times over.

FAKE A BLOG. As I mentioned in Chapter 5, blogging is a huge commitment. But you don't have to start a blog yourself to drive additional traffic to your website. Instead, you could publish a monthly or quarterly e-newsletter using software like ConstantContact.com (starts at $15 a month for a 500-email list; as I write this, there's a free 60-day trial offered). Or you could write an op-ed piece for your local newspaper or industry publication, or write a guest blog post for a well-read blog in your field. Don't just write a public service announcement for your freelance business; instead, write about a hot trend in the field and offer as many tips as you can. Be sure to include your web address at the end of any articles or guest blog posts you do so people know how to reach you.

PAMPER YOUR CLIENTS. Photographer Anne Ruthmann spends all her marketing dollars on complimentary, handbag-size brag books she makes for her clients of her favorite images from their wedding day.

"I could say up front that it's included in their package, but it's way more fun for them to be surprised and excited about it," she explains. It's also a nice touch that lands her a lot of referrals.

While many freelancers send their clients cards, candy, booze, and other treats during the year-end holidays, you can really give them something to remember by sending them a book for their birthday, bath salts for Valentine's Day, Girl Scout cookies in March, or any other offbeat gift during an unexpected time of the year. Just be sure your client doesn't work for an organization that has a no-gifts policy; I recently had two clients at a Fortune 500 company politely decline gift certificates I sent them for this very reason. (Awkward.)

THROW AN EVENT. "The press won't write about an unknown artist, but they'll write about something folks can have fun at," Molly Crabapple says. The woman knows of what she speaks. The biweekly burlesque drawing event she launched in 2005, Dr. Sketchy's Anti-Art School, spread her name around the globe and landed her hundreds of press write-ups. Like an art class on acid, Dr. Sketchy's has spread to fifty cities around the world, became a book in 2006, and now covers the cost of Molly's New York rent check each month.

If you want to throw an event, team up with your fellow freelancers (including one with prior event-planning experience), get people drunk (or at least feed them cupcakes), and amuse your audience with your talents. When throwing an event, bring sign-up sheets to collect names for your mailing list, postcards featuring your web address, and any products you have to hawk. Go for the soft sell: Everyone expects a quick announcement that there's merch, literature, and the like on the back table; no one wants to hear a thirty-five-minute PSA though, unless it's highly entertaining.

NOTIFY THE MEDIA. Don't wait till the eve of your book reading, art opening, or concert to contact the press. One to three months' lead time is what they need. Triple that for print magazines. Likewise, don't trouble a reporter unless you have a really juicy story or exciting event to share. While thrilling to you, chances are your local Lois Lane won't care that you just celebrated your one-year anniversary as a freelance interior designer—unless you're Melinda Gates's designer and have some tips to share on how you snagged one of the richest women in the world as a customer. For all the suggestions you could want about writing press releases, pitching reporters, and spinning an angle that news hounds are likely to appreciate, see PublicityHound.com and PublicityInsider.com.

The Work You Really Want to Do

I once saw actor John Cusack being interviewed on TV about why he makes movies like *Must Love Dogs* when he clearly could devote his time to more worthy projects like *High Fidelity* and *Being John Malkovich*.

"I do one for them, then one for me," he said, referring to how he alternates between supercommercial big-budget studio flicks and the smaller indie projects that really turn his crank, so he can afford to make the films he wants to make. Sometimes, ole Johnny said, he even gets lucky and one of his commercial films winds up being a meaningful project he's actually proud of.

By now you know that I'm a fan of juggling pays-the-bills freelance work with the lower-paying creative work that you love most. This isn't the proverbial sell-out—it's survival. Don't listen to anyone who tries to tell you otherwise. As the alternatives are to get a day job or live on a park bench, I'll take this balancing act any day of the week.

"I don't have a trust fund," says writer Meghan Daum. "I don't have parents who give me money. I don't think people realize that a lot of people who are quote-unquote self-employed don't have money from secret money sources. And if you don't, you have to do these other things, and there's no point in being ashamed of it."

Besides, do you really think any painter, folksinger, or novelist tells herself, "I'm gonna make damned sure I never have enough money to sleep anywhere but on my best friend's futon for the next decade or vacation anywhere other than the nearest rest stop on I-90"? Doubtful.

"There are so few ways musicians have been aptly compensated for their craft that it makes my heart soar when I hear that great artists

I know have licensed a song to a car or insurance company," says New York singer/songwriter Erika Simonian, who supplements the income she earns from performing and selling CDs by bartending in an organic restaurant two nights a week. "Frankly, it's my dream to sell one of my songs to another performer or license my music for a commercial."

But financial peace of mind isn't the only benefit of adding some corporate, commercial, or commissioned work to your schedule. You're also getting paid to refine your skills, and you're getting your work seen and heard by a far wider audience. In addition, you get a breather from cranking out that creative gold day in and day out. Because believe it or not, an overload of hours at the keyboard, easel, or engineering table, even on a dream project, is a surefire recipe for burning out and losing your creative mojo. Yes, Virginia, even that "living the dream" work you once coveted can become a mercenary nightmare if you overdo it.

"Sometimes the things that I like to do wind up getting clogged with deadlines and then it starts to become something that I just have to do—even things that I wound up loving and had a lot of creative control over," says illustrator Ellen Forney. "That's part of the artistic process: to feel so much pressure to do what it is that you're doing well that you're just hating it. Sometimes it's hard to remember that you have to go through that in order to make your best work."

On the flip side, it's easy to go to the opposite extreme, working 99.9 percent of your time on pay-the-bills projects alone. So how do you make room in your schedule for the work you really want to do? There's only one way: by making it a priority, just as you would for exercising, meeting friends, or buying groceries.

"One really has to say, 'This is the time where I am going to make creative work and I am not going to do my laundry or clean up dust bunnies,'" says illustrator Nina Frenkel. "The longer I stay out of this practice of making time for my own art, the harder it is to reinstitute a practice—it becomes almost scary, unnecessarily so. The only way through this is to get my butt in the chair and do it."

In other words, the longer you stray, the tougher it is to coax yourself back into the work that feels like play. If you're not one of those freakishly regimented, compartmentalization-happy folks who can do two hours of creative work at the start of each workday without fail (don't worry, I'm not either), don't despair. You have options. The most common is to build a couple of short stints in the creative hot seat into your weekly schedule—thirty minutes when junior's down for his nap, an hour before you hit the hay, whatever you've got—so doing your own work becomes habit forming. I do suggest making an actual appointment with yourself, though (even setting your Outlook calendar or cell phone to remind you), so you don't forget or let it slide. And this will of course mean scaling back on money work by 5, 10, or 25 percent, depending on how much time and income you can spare.

While embroiled in an all-encompassing stretch of pay-the-bills work, at least take a few minutes a week to record, jot down, or sketch all the creative ideas that come to you. (Trust me, you will have them.) Most likely, you'll crave these small snippets of brainstorming time more than ever. "While I haven't been making a lot of my own pieces I have been sketchbooking up a storm," says Nina, who's been managing a team of subcontractors on the same beefy animation project for the past eighteen months. "It's been a place to explore ideas or put notes to self— 'Here's an idea, here's an image'—and to plant seeds for later when the space and time is there."

If you're juggling more balls than a Barnum & Bailey circus clown, when you go to change gears from your money to your creative work, you may experience a little problem I like to call "How in the hell am I supposed to have a crazy one-night stand in my boring old marriage bed?" syndrome. Sometimes changing your workspace when shifting from a bread-and-butter job to a dream project can help shake loose the cobwebs; for me, grabbing my notepad or laptop and relocating to another room in the house or to a café usually does the trick.

And if, like me, you're a bit of an ADD case who, at times, has trouble keeping the pedal to the creative metal for even one damn hour, find yourself a study buddy or three who'll swap creative projects with you and offer suggestions, encouragement, and tough love as needed. Pick a concrete deadline to work toward—a contest, a grant, a residency application, a gallery's call for visual artists, an anthology looking for submissions. Invent bite-size challenges you can mutually strive toward—developing one new cartoon character a month, publishing a poem in a lit journal in each of the fifty states before the decade's out, coming up with a new apron pattern for Mother's Day. Nothing lights a fire under my backside like an email from someone in my freelance posse saying, "I wrote my five hundred words/spent my hour at the easel/practiced three songs today—how about you?"

Making time for the work you really want to do is about making choices and compromising when you have to. Some freelancers budget an afternoon or day each week for tapping their creative vein, like web designer Colleen Lynn, who, as you saw in Chapter 17, reserves part of each Friday for her creative work. Others flit from three-month bread-and-butter gig to three-month creative stint and back again. And some get the bulk of their annual creative work done during a few weeks a year spent at an artists' retreat. I've tried all these ways, and after more than a decade, I'm still trying to strike the perfect balance of cash flow and creativity.

The key is to avoid driving yourself—and everyone within earshot—crazy by wailing about how broke you are, not to mention quashing your creative drive with all that financial terror. There are dozens of recipes for striking that balance between art and commerce. So experiment. Mix and match. And don't be afraid to get creative about how you finance and make time for getting your creative kicks. Because the only person who can tell you what strategy will work best for you is you.

epilogue

I Am Freelance (and So Can You!)

As you work to get your freelance life on track, a number of external forces may conspire to keep your creative soul train from leaving the station. For one thing, there will be all manner of naysayers, as there are any time anyone endeavors to do something unconventional (say, invent their own job). Don't let these killjoys derail your dream of working solo. Instead, make it your mission in life to see just how fast you can prove them wrong.

If I had listened to my family, my college advisers, and even many of the friends I've made over the years, you wouldn't be reading this book right now—mainly because I'd be working some full-time office job instead of working from home in three-day-old jammies. Instead, I'm with artist Nikki McClure, who says, "To me it's about making your own economy, and that's about disregarding the common way of making money."

Not everyone will be a naysayer. In fact, many people will be excited, encouraging, and brimming with ideas about how you should pursue the freelance path, from your postal carrier to your cat. They'll all have multiple unsolicited suggestions about the "right way" to run a business of one. But just because your aunt Barb saw Oprah say that her BFF Gayle told her that her accountant says that you need to incorporate your business from day one and hire an army of life coaches to tell you how to grow your creative empire doesn't mean you should listen.

There are more obstacles out there, too—some of them lurking within, including those pesky business mores we think we're supposed to abide by simply because they existed at some point in time, like back when people traveled by horse and buggy. For example, I used to think it was more professional to not let on that I was calling clients or story sources at a desk just twenty paces from my bed (for some reason,

211

people do ask where I work all the time). Now if it comes up, I say I'm freelancing from my home office.

Likewise, I've gone from sweating the fact that my dog has a nasty habit of launching into a barking fit when I'm on a conference call or being interviewed on live radio to laughing it off with a joke about my low-rent security team. And while the mompreneurs I've talked to over the years do their darnedest to make sure their kids aren't screeching in the background during mommy's business calls, they don't try to hide the fact that they're parents from their clients. In other words, being human is the new black.

But not knowing how real we can get with our clients isn't the only thing that trips us up as freelancers. There are all those outmoded business management "shoulds" to contend with too: We should do whatever it takes to make a mint. We should spend a fortune on advertising. We should expand like there's no tomorrow. We should have our exit strategy planned from the get-go. We should be hardcore, ruthless, skeptical of so much as saying hello to the competition.

"My biggest challenges are fighting the things in my own head about the way a businesswoman should be: that I need to behave like a man or my perception of a man, when in fact all my business is built on my ability to have relationships," says Wendy Merrill, owner of WAM Marketing Group. "It's not a cutthroat, dog-eat-dog, cut-'em-off-at-the-knees world."

Sarah Haynes of The Spitfire Agency has also rallied against tradition. "I could maximize my earnings by limiting my business to a few core competencies and doing them over and over again for the same people, but that would limit my love of my job," she says. "I get bored doing the same thing every time. I like to prove that new things can be done. Once I've done something a few times, I'll usually run off and do something else."

So don't worry about what Martha Stewart or Steve Jobs would do—here's a better list of freelancer goals to aspire to: Be true to yourself. Work when and how and with whom you want. Treat your clients well. Charge what you're worth. Keep setting new goals for yourself. Branch out into new niches. Learn new tricks and acquire new skills. Plant your ass in the chair and make time to refine your craft. Read interviews with your career heroes. Follow the news of your field. Take classes on anything that excites you. Go to book readings, art exhibits, rock shows, or whatever else inspires you. Rub elbows with like-minded indie professionals at happy hours and conferences. Make new freelance friends— even with competitors. Encourage, cajole, and collaborate. Celebrate your wins. Learn from your defeats, but don't dwell on them. And above all, remember to have fun.

If I thought it would help, I'd ask you to do some lame exercise in which you visualize yourself into becoming the next Diablo Cody or Amy Sedaris. I'd tell you not to worry about stiffing your cell phone carrier, mortgage lender, or the IRS or sweat the fact that your only client is *Pest Control Technology* magazine. If I thought it would help, I'd tell you to burn some sage, chant "I am successful, I am successful, I am successful" a thousand times fast, and visualize your checking account filling with shekels as your inbox overflows with freelance job offers from Oprah Winfrey herself. "Never mind the home foreclosure notice your bank sent you or the repo company that just showed up to haul off your car," I'd insist. "Let nothing, *nothing*—not even a two-year jail sentence for tax evasion—distract you from all your invaluable chanting, sage burning, and visualization exercises."

I could say that, but I won't. Because ignoring reality and embracing the woo-woo approach to work is not going to get you where you want to go. In fact, it's going to get you a ticket to nowhere fast.

While I'm a fan of positive thinking, the reality is that growing a kick-ass freelance business requires a healthy dose of perseverance and chutzpah. Building a solid, steady client base takes time, patience, resilience. Ditto for branching out into a new creative niche—travel photography, T-shirt silk-screening, teak furniture building—or climbing to the next rung of the self-employment ladder. If there were a magic, one-size-fits-all silver bullet, everyone would quit and start freelancing tomorrow with a deskful of contracts from the likes of *The New Yorker* and Barneys and Paramount Pictures.

I'd be lying if I said I don't get bored or demoralized from time to time. Or that I've never fantasized about taking up something more predictable, like digging graves or driving the truck that paints the white lines down the highway. Most freelancers do. But like all the freelancers you've met in this book, I'm hooked on being mistress of my own career destiny. Succeed or fail, at least I'm cracking my own whip and playing by my own rules.

If ever I start to lose the faith, I get up from my desk and get the heck out of the office. As I change from my "work pajamas" into clothes a person can actually wear in public, I remind myself that I'm lucky to have a job I like 95 percent of the time, which according to the sobering stats that business think tanks throw at us each year is more than most people can say. Then I dance around the living room awhile, take my dog out for a stroll, and catch dinner and a movie with a friend.

When I get to work the next morning, there might be a nice note in my inbox from a satisfied client or a check in my PO box. But if not, it won't matter. What matters is that I'm doing what I've wanted to do since I was an eight-year-old in pigtails writing essays about Pocahontas and gluing together dioramas of dinosaurs—I'm making a living making stuff. You might even say I'm making tracks.

These are a few of my favorite freelance things, from books to web communities to professional associations to artist retreats and back again. To keep this list under a thousand pages, I'll do my best to limit it to industry-agnostic resources. If you want to zero in on resources specific to dog groomers or gardening consultants or any other freelance field, let your search engine do the walking.

GETCHER FREELANCE TIPS HERE

www.anti9to5guide.com. Color me shameless, but I couldn't not mention my own blog on self-employment and alternative careers, could I?

www.creativepro.com. Mostly geared toward visual creatives, this site is exploding with all the usual web stuff: news, articles, reviews, blogs, et cetera.

http://freelancefolder.com and **http://freelanceswitch.com.** Two of the biggest freelancing blogs out there. I don't always agree with each article, but I savor the variety of opinions and the wisdom of many of the seasoned pros who comment. Don't miss the job listings and forums on FreelanceSwitch.

www.mediabistro.com. If you're a media worker who has never heard of this site, time to pull your head out of the sand. On it, you'll find news, interviews, blogs, tips, events, classes, forums, and probably about 250 other things I'm forgetting.

http://webworkerdaily.com. If you're one of those people who love to read about tech tools and productivity tips for home-based workers, you will totally dig this site.

GET TO KNOW THE RIGHT PEOPLE

http://biznik.com. A social networking site with the tagline "Business networking that doesn't suck"—how can you resist? The marketing articles and tips posted by members always keep me coming back for more.

www.freelancersunion.org. Not only does the Freelancers Union (free to join) offer health insurance in thirty-one states (at the time of this writing), meetup groups, and job listings, they're advocating like crazy to land us better insurance, tax, and unemployment rights and laws.

www.the-efa.org. The Editorial Freelancers Association offers communication pros online classes, web resources ranging from pricing guidelines to sample contracts, access to job listings (for a nominal fee), health insurance in several states, and more.

www.gag.org. The Graphic Artists Guild advocates for the copyrights of visual creatives, offers contract assistance and job listings to members, and has a dozen chapters throughout the country that host workshops and schmoozefests.

There are scores of other trade-specific professional associations out there—American Federation of Musicians (www.afm.org), Association of Independents in Radio (www.airmedia.org), National Writers Union (www.nwu.org), Professional Photographers of America (www.ppa.com), Women in Film (www.wif.org), and on and on and on. These groups offer everything from contract advocacy help and affordable health plans to classes, job listings, website hosting, regional happy hours, and online industry news and contract tips. Ask your freelance pals for their recommendations of local and national associations. Be sure to check out the benefits an organization offers before you fork over that $50 to $300 annual membership fee.

SHOW ME THE MONEY

On My Own Two Feet: A Modern Girl's Guide to Personal Finance, by Manisha Thakor and Sharon Kedar, Adams Media, 2007. After reading this invaluable book, you will never again mindlessly charge $500 of clothes you can't afford. Instead, you'll have a savings account, a rainy day fund, and a retirement account, and you'll be well on your way to having all your financial ducks in a row.

Why Women Earn Less: How to Make What You're Really Worth, by Mikelann Valterra, Career Press, 2004. Written by an author/business coach after my own heart! This book tells you how to get over the notion that poverty is noble and start asking for more money. For additional tips and resources on negotiating freelance rates, see Mikelann online at www.womenearning.com.

BUSINESS PLANNING FOR BEGINNERS

The Anti 9-to-5 Guide: Practical Career Advice for Women Who Think Outside the Cube, by Michelle Goodman, Seal Press, 2007. Okay, I know I'm biased, but if you need additional guidance on finding your so-called passion, starting a creative venture on the side, transitioning from a conventional day job to temp or flex work, and making sure you're covered financially every step of the way, this book is for you.

The Boss of You: Everything a Woman Needs to Know to Start, Run, and Maintain Her Own Business, by Emira Mears and Lauren Bacon, Seal Press, 2008. Have a question about budgeting, branding, finding the right customers, hiring employees, and just about anything else start-up related? These two savvy small business owners will give you the inside dish.

www.nolo.com. Free online legal advice for those who don't speak legalese, from forming an LLC to protecting your copyrights. Oodles of trade-specific start-up and copyright books and downloadable forms you can buy (*License & Merchandise Creative Art, The Legal Guide to Web*

& *Software Development,* and so on). Don't miss the podcasts and the copyrights blog.

www.score.org. How do I love SCORE? Let me count the ways: Free business plan, expense, and budgeting templates on their website. Dozens of free articles on everything from start-up considerations to business expansion. Free online or face-to-face mentoring with seasoned business pros. Chapters throughout the country that offer practical, low-cost "Business 101" workshops. What's not to love?

RATES AND CONTRACTS AND COPYRIGHTS—OH MY!

Consultant & Independent Contractor Agreements, Fifth Edition, by Stephen Fishman, Nolo, 2005. A legal eagle and champion of indie business owners breaks down all you need to know about the contracts you sign with clients and those you sign when you hire other freelancers (subcontractors). As a bonus, the companion CD contains contract templates you can use.

The Graphic Artists Guild Handbook: Pricing & Ethical Guidelines, Twelfth Edition, Allworth Press, 2008. My illustrator, animator, and design pals swear by this one. And if you join the Guild, you get a copy free. Nice!

What to Charge: Pricing Strategies for Freelancers and Consultants, by Laurie Lewis, Aletheia Publications, 2000. If you want to ensure you're charging enough for your work and negotiating as effectively as you can, pick up a copy of this book. Great examples of price structures and negotiations that worked for some freelancers, as well as those that backfired.

www.copyright.gov. The U.S. Copyright Office offers comprehensive info you can actually understand about protecting your work. If you want to register your work with the Library of Congress, you can download the forms from this site.

www.keepyourcopyrights.org. A bunch of legal profs at Columbia Law School put together this site so we mere mortals could better decipher our contracts. Great examples of sample contracts, as well as good, bad, and downright worse-than-unfair clauses.

www.starvingartistslaw.com. Who are these wonderful people that compiled link after link of "Copyrights 101" articles, and will they mind if I give them a sloppy wet kiss? Even more lovely is the fact that they've compiled a list of North American legal clinics offering free contract and business advice to creative types.

DEATH AND TAXES

Working for Yourself: Law & Taxes for Independent Contractors, Freelancers & Consultants, Seventh Edition, by Stephen Fishman, Nolo, 2008. More ass-saving advice from every freelancer's favorite attorney and our friends at Nolo.com.

www.irs.gov. While nothing takes the place of the advice of a good accountant, the IRS site is surprisingly informative and easy to navigate. If, however, you're dying to hear a recorded greeting that says "Welcome to the IRS!" give the feds a call with your questions: (800) 829-4933. If your income is $40,000 or less, the IRS has a Volunteer Income Tax Assistance (VITA) program that can help you prepare your tax return. Call (800) 829-1040 for locations.

www.turbotax.com. Besides offering freelance-friendly tax preparation software, TurboTax offers a bunch of helpful tax tips, calculators, and advice on its website.

INSURE YOUR HIDE

www.ahirc.org and **www.healthinsuranceinfo.net.** Both sites list individual and group health insurance options available in each of the United States. Both are goldmines of information.

www.ehealthinsurance.com. This site makes comparison shopping for a health plan a cinch. But if you want someone to break down what you're really getting with those monthly premiums, see an insurance agent (free).

www.nahu.org. The National Association of Health Underwriters lists thousands of licensed insurance agents who can help hunt down the best health policy for you.

BLOGGING 101

The cheapest way to start a blog is via a platform like www.blogger.com (free), http://wordpress.com (free), or www.typepad.com ($5 a month; two-week free trial). But if you want your own domain name (www. myradsite.com, as opposed to http://myradsite.wordpress.com) and extra blogging capabilities, get thee to http://wordpress.org, download the blogging software they tell you to download (easy), and sign up for a web hosting service (about $100 to $200 a year).

WordPress for Dummies, by Lisa Sabin-Wilson, For Dummies, 2007. If you're a baby blogger, there's a lot to digest at the outset. This book makes doing all of the above with WordPress—my blogging platform recommendation—even easier.

www.bloggingbasics101.com. Tagline: "Where there are no stupid questions!" All I can say is, I wish I'd known about this site when I first started blogging.

www.copyblogger.com and **www.problogger.net.** Want to write snappier blog posts, boost your blog traffic, and maybe even make a little cash in the process? CopyBlogger and ProBlogger can help.

VIRTUAL ASSISTANCE, ANYONE?

If you need help getting your admin done, these organizations can hook you up with a qualified professional: International Virtual Assistants

Association (www.ivaa.org), Virtual Assistance Chamber of Commerce (www.virtualassistantnetworking.com), and Virtual Assistants Networking Association (www.vanetworking.com).

GIVE YOURSELF A CREATIVE KICK IN THE PANTS

www.artistcommunities.org. Find an artist retreat or residency to apply for. Nothing beats getting away from every last obligation in your life and having the time and space—usually in some fairytalelike setting—to just make stuff.

www.shawguides.com. Landscape painting lessons in Tuscany! Writing workshops on the Pacific coastline! Travel photography training in Zanzibar! If you like to mix travel with professional development, don't miss the listings on this site.

How to Become a Famous Writer Before You're Dead: Your Words in Print and Your Name in Lights, by Ariel Gore, Three Rivers Press, 2007. Like Anne Lamott's classic *Bird by Bird: Some Instructions on Writing and Life* (Anchor, 1995), this book's "get off your duff and do it now" message will hit home for freelancers of all trades, as will the fearless, DIY shameless self-promo tips.

The Creative Habit: Learn It and Use It for Life, by Twyla Tharp, Simon & Schuster, 2003. Still haven't gotten off your duff? This legendary choreographer can help you muster up the discipline and cultivate a lifelong creative routine.

The War of Art: Break Through the Blocks and Win Your Inner Creative Battles, by Steven Pressfield, Warner Books, 2003. I owe the fact that I got up the nerve to start writing the book you hold in your hands to Steven Pressfield's brilliant take on why we procrastinate and how to fight it. Enough said.

acknowledgments

Roll credits!

Before I go to Disneyland (i.e., sleep for the next nine days), there are a few people I'd like to thank for their generous help in getting this book off my laptop and into your hands:

Props to Lisa Owens and my Editorial Freelancers Association students for giving me a reason to think long and hard about how to cultivate a kickass freelance business. A big shout-out to Brooke Warner at Seal Press, who championed this project and tirelessly coaxed me to the finish line. Thanks also to Seal heroes Megan Cooney, Andie East, Elizabeth Mathews, and Dylan Wooters for working their bookmaking magic. And special thanks to Elizabeth Wales for her wise counsel and invaluable big-picture advice.

A number of friends and colleagues contributed their time and expertise to this project as well. Diane Mapes read every blasted chapter, talked me off the ledge repeatedly, and remains the best damned writing coach I know. Lauren Bacon, Maria Gargiulo, Emira Mears, and Jill Rothenberg offered invaluable feedback when I was stuck. Money whiz kids Bill Ehardt, Manisha Thakor, and Rhebe Greenwald kindly reviewed the financial chapters of the book. Small business advisers Michael Graham of Washington Lawyers for the Arts, Elizabeth Mance of Accountability Services, and Mikelann Valterra of Women's Earning Institute shared their priceless insights. Molly Bennett, Lara Eve Feltin, Angela Fountas, Nina Frenkel, Jane Hodges, Kurt Stephan, Julie van Amerongen, and the Biznik and Digital Eve communities offered introductions to a wealth of top-notch interviewees. Thank you all for so generously lending a hand.

My undying gratitude also goes out to the following folks: The Hedgebrook crew, for the lovely Whidbey Island retreat just when I needed it. I can't think of a more perfect place to begin writing a book.

My understanding mom, for bringing me homemade soup. My sister, Naomi, for calling every few days to make sure I was still alive. My ultra-patient boyfriend, Greg, for bringing me the biggest slice of chocolate cake I've ever seen and letting me hibernate for weeks on end. And everyone else who emailed missives of encouragement and baited me with finish-line promises of baked goods, mystery gifts, and dinners out with the rest of humanity. Sloppy kisses to the whole lot of you.

Finally, a big fat hat tip to the readers of the Anti9to5Guide.com blog for asking so many fantastic questions about the so-called freelance life. Hopefully I've answered them all. My heartfelt thanks also goes out to the clients who've kept me gainfully employed over the years—I'm grateful for your contributions to the roof over my head, and the material. And most important, I'd like to thank the fearless freelancers (and the clients who hire them) who put up with my nosy questions and shared their hard-won tips and war stories with me for this book. A roaring standing ovation to you all.

the author

M ichelle Goodman is author of *The Anti 9-to-5 Guide: Practical Career Advice for Women Who Think Outside the Cube*, an irreverent handbook for aspiring cubicle expats. Her articles and essays about alternative careers, human mating rituals, and cultural trends have graced media outlets such as ABCNews.com, CNN.com, Salon.com, *The Seattle Times, BUST, Bitch,* and *The Bark,* and have appeared in the anthologies *Single State of the Union: Single Women Speak Out on Life, Love, and the Pursuit of Happiness* and *The Moment of Truth: Women's Funniest Romantic Catastrophes*. In her fifteen years as a full-time freelancer, she's had the opportunity to wrangle text on computer games, marital aids, dog pajamas, home colonics, and just about anything else that can be sold. She lives in Seattle with her eighty-pound lapdog, Buddy. For more scoop on the so-called freelance life, visit her blog at Anti9to5Guide.com.

Selected Titles from Seal Press

For more than thirty years,
Seal Press has published groundbreaking books.
By women. For women.
Visit our website at www.sealpress.com.
Check out the Seal Press blog at www.sealpress.com/blog.

The Anti 9-to-5 Guide: Practical Career Advice for Women Who Think Outside the Cube, by Michelle Goodman. $14.95, 1-58005-186-3. Escape the wage-slave trap of your cubicle with Goodman's hip career advice on creating your dream job and navigating the work world without compromising your aspirations.

The Boss of You: Everything A Woman Needs to Know to Start, Run, and Maintain Her Own Business, by Emira Mears & Lauren Bacon. $15.95, 1-58005-236-3. Provides women entrepreneurs the advice, guidance, and straightforward how-to's they need to start, run, and maintain a business.

Own It!: The Ups and Downs of Homebuying for Women Who Go It Alone, by Jennifer Musselman. $15.95, 1-58005-230-4. This mix of guidebook how-to and personal narrative covers the how-to's and hiccups of homebuying for women braving the process alone.

The Money Therapist: A Woman's Guide to Creating A Healthy Financial Life, by Marcia Brixey. $15.95, 1-58005-216-9. Offers women of every financial strata the tools they need to manage their money, set attainable budget goals, get out of debt, and create a healthy financial life.

Job Hopper: The Checkered Career of a Down-Market Dilettante, by Ayun Halliday. $14.95, 1-58005-130-8. Halliday, quickly becoming one of America's funniest writers, chronicles her hilarious misadventures in the working world.

Getting Unstuck Without Coming Unglued: A Woman's Guide to Unblocking Creativity, by Susan O'Doherty, Ph.D. $14.95, 1-58005-206-1. This encouraging and practical book is about understanding blocks in the creative process and getting to the bottom of what causes them.